I Have a Secret

H Bird

authorHOUSE®

AuthorHouse™
1663 Liberty Drive
Bloomington, IN 47403
www.authorhouse.com
Phone: 1 (800) 839-8640

Published by AuthorHouse 06/28/2017

ISBN: 978-1-5246-9828-7 (sc)
ISBN: 978-1-5246-9830-0 (hc)
ISBN: 978-1-5246-9829-4 (e)

Library of Congress Control Number: 2017910111

Print information available on the last page.

Contents

Chapter 1

I am wrapped in my warm cocoon of serenity, away from the unpredictable world, the confusion, the anger. Breathing the warm, almost thick, smell of old leather cracked and turned yellow by age. Bumping and creaking on the rusty old springs, over small stones on the roadside. The rhythmic lurch to the right from the bent wheel of this well used buggy. I am being pushed by my ten-year old sister Amanda, who is much too young to be responsible for such a tiny, 9-month-old baby. Walking with us, to get out of our Mother's hair, is my middle sister Corinne. At age 4, she is already much too opinionated for her own good. She is such a free spirit but, in this world of survival, no one has time to appreciate her incredible sense of wonderment.

Suddenly clanging and thudding sounds intrude on my sleep! "Quiet Scott, you'll wake the baby! Take those noisy pails and Cocoa way up ahead of us," ordered Amanda as firmly as her squeaky child voice could muster.

We are on a raspberry picking Safari, to the other side of the neighbor's fence. Scott, my seven-year-old brother, is carrying our equipment. Cocoa, our family dog, would protect us from anything except water. Even though his Labrador retriever half made him a great swimmer, his cocker spaniel half made his fur so thick, long and curly that it would soak up too much water and suck him under. There was not much worry of this here though, as there were no lakes for quite a distance.

Just as Amanda had expected, Scott's ruckus woke me and I started wailing. "Oh great. Now I'll have to push Hanna all the way home and Mum will be so mad!" lamented Amanda. It may sound like she was over dramatizing her predicament, but it really was no easy chore to push that cumbersome buggy through the foot-tall grasses of the field. Mum was always so tired when she was doing all of our laundry. She had to do it every second or third day in the old wringer washer that took constant supervision. It was heavy, manual labour lifting the soaked clothes out of the water and feeding them through the wringers. Each time she did laundry, Mum would remember how her own mother's beautiful long hair had been caught in the wringers and ripped from her scalp, never to grow the same again. Then Mum would have to carry all the clothes to the yard to hang them on the clothes line. The broken wooden and metal pins would sometimes let go from the weight and send all of her hard work falling to the dirt below to become laundry again for tomorrow.

"My goodness, what's all that noise about?" cooed our Mother's voice.

"I'm so sorry, Mum. It was Scott's fault for waking her up" apologized Amanda.

Mum answered as she lifted me from the buggy, "Not to worry, babies are meant to wake up at the worst times. You go along and fetch us some of those marvelous berries. We're going to need something for dessert. I'll manage this little bumpkin."

I believe I knew, from the time my Mother carried me in her womb, that I would be dearly loved and the glue to hold our family together. It was for this reason, as she held me, that I stopped crying. She then changed my wet clothing. More laundry for tomorrow! She laid me back in the snug buggy in the yard for a nap before walking into the kitchen to get the basket of wet clothes for hanging on the line outside. As she bent down to pick up the basket, our blue budgie Joey, landed on her shoulder to steal a ride out into the warm summer sunshine. People were amazed that the bird never flew away when they did this, but to me it just seemed natural that two such gentle creatures should want to stay together.

I awoke from my nap to giggles and a gentle slurping sound. My siblings were all crowded around our kitchen table. It was the old, arborite kind. Red with chrome legs. They were relishing the simple flavors of raspberries with sugar and canned milk. It wasn't often they could afford to have dessert and this was a special moment to be savored and remembered.

The back door opened and in came my eldest brother Pat, short for Patrick. At only thirteen years old he had finished his two paper routes for the day. The money he earned was needed to help feed our family. Mum quickly dished up his dinner of baked beans and fried spam with a glass of powdered skim milk. He always enjoyed his dinner, because he would be so hungry, and tonight there was dessert!

As he was happily dishing up his bowl of raspberries and reaching for the sugar…BAM! That same tranquil backdoor that opened to let Pat in, now became an instrument of anger and terror as it was thrust inward, banging the wall so hard that the handle imbedded in the plaster. Cocoa leapt to his feet from his resting place behind the old oil stove. He was barking and growling at his master who had barged into this once peaceful abode. In running to meet this intruder, Cocoa was greeted with a swift kick in the ribs to shove him out the door which was then slammed shut behind him.

"Chad please," sighed Mum as she went to check how the dog was, only to be pushed to the floor as she reached for the doorknob.

Once again, I was screaming. "Take the baby and go into the other room," Pat whispered sternly to the kids. They knew from experience, to obey quickly.

I was being pushed in my buggy from the room as Pat's bowl of raspberries was flung skyward by a swing of our father's arm. Amanda lifted me from my buggy in her shaking arms and the four of us crept up to our rooms while the storm raged on below.

I don't remember too much from my really early childhood, and some say maybe that's for the best. Over all I think that we were basically happy with a sprinkling of terrible moments. I know that we owe a lot of thanks to Pat, who shielded us from the worst of it. His life had been filled with our father belittling, rejecting and hitting him and he wanted better for us. He behaved more like a man, now at thirteen, than our father did. This probably made Pat a target for much of the abuse he suffered, as our father would have seen this too.

Chapter 2

My next memory is from about age three. I remember watching my brothers building their wooden, soapbox, racecars out of scraps of wood and old buggy wheels. They were pretty impressive looking and could really pick up speed going down our steep hill. I wasn't allowed to ride in them, so soon lost interest and went to play by the stream. It was actually a 6-inch-wide ditch but I could watch the clear water babbling over the rocks and grass for hours. I loved to float little twigs and splash my hands in the water. Amanda would be helping Mum make bread or, sometimes, even cookies. Corinne would be playing house at her friend's. Her friend had much nicer toys and dolls there.

That night we all gathered in my brothers' room to watch the electric train go around and around. I felt something warm and wet on my lip when Corinne shouted, "Hanna has a nose bleed again!" Apparently, I got them quite often. Some people said they thought it was from the stress I was living under. Not knowing when or if my father would come home and if he would beat my Mum or brother again when he did.

At age four I remember my dad coming home in his shiny car. He asked me if I wanted to go for a ride in it!! WOW! I knew I had not been in a moving car before and I was so excited! I had to ask my Mum but surely, she would let me, I thought. This was about the most exciting thing that had ever happened to me!

"Oh, but we were just going to have lunch," Mum said. "And I was going to take you for a ride in my race buggy," piped in Pat.

"She could do that stuff anytime," answered my Dad.

"No, Chad, that's not a good idea," retorted Mum.

"To hell with that she's my kid and I'm taking her!" he replied.

I was so happy to go that it didn't matter that Mum and Pat were

4

running after the car looking very concerned. I would see them after my ride. It never occurred to my young mind that they may have a reason to not want me to go.

The trees and building tops sailed right by my window, it was so exciting. I couldn't see the people or sidewalks, as I was too short to have a good view, but it didn't matter. I was in a moving car! Then we came to a stop and my Dad got out saying, "I'll just be a few minutes. Be good." Of course, I'd be good. It wasn't all the time I got to ride in a moving car.

I sat up on my knees so I could look outside and watch the people walking by. There were kids at the park playing ball, ladies pushing shopping carts and dogs chasing cats. After a while, I got bored watching them, so I moved over to pretend that I was driving. It was such fun! Then I honked the horn by accident. I was so scared I would be in trouble that I jumped over the seat into the back and hid on the floor. I think I fell asleep down there because when I got up it was all different outside. The darkness was moving in. The kids were gone from the park and there wasn't anyone on the sidewalk anymore. Now I started wishing that my Dad would come back. I was getting hungry and I needed to go to the bathroom. I kept looking for something to entertain me while waiting. I moved from the back floor to the seat and then to the front seat and back again. I was bouncing on the seat, holding my bottom so I wouldn't wet my pants. I wanted to go home so badly that I started to cry. I think that I cried myself to sleep again as I was awakened by a lady knocking on the car window. She was asking me if I was alright.

It was pitch dark outside and my pants were wet. I was really afraid of that strange lady trying to take me. Luckily my Dad appeared. His clothes were all messed up and he was walking as if he was dancing. That lady started yelling at him right away, saying something about the child in the car. He said that he didn't know anything about any child in the car and I know he was telling the truth because as he unlocked the door he was very surprised to see me.

He muttered some words to me as he fell in behind the steering wheel, but I couldn't understand what he said. I just sat on the back seat as quiet as a mouse hoping that he would forget I was there. I was scared that I would get a spanking for having wet my pants, so I stayed very quiet.

The car smelled badly from my pee and something else both acrid and sour. I was thinking I might throw up, when he suddenly stopped the car to throw up himself. More muttering, that I could not understand, then on we went again. The next time we stopped, I heard my Mum and Pat's voices. They were shouting and calling my name and they didn't sound very happy. I guess they were still mad at me that I went for the drive and now they were yelling at Dad too. It was all my fault and I was ashamed of my wet pants. My Mummy was hugging me and crying as she lifted me out of the car. She passed me to Pat, who carried me to Amanda, who then gave me a bath. The warm water felt nice, as did the soft pjs and warm glass of milk afterwards. I couldn't understand why I didn't get in trouble for my wet pants, but I was glad I didn't. I promised out loud to never go in the car again. I was so sorry. It felt so good to be home that I drifted off easily to sleep, despite all the yelling downstairs.

The next morning, I came downstairs and there was a new piece of furniture in the living room. I was sleepy still and didn't even notice it when I walked by. My family was laughing because it was a big surprise to all of them. They thought we could never afford a television! I had never even heard about television before this.

"Come and I'll show you how it works," said Pat. He showed me how to pull out the little knob to turn it on. Then we waited while the light inside warmed up and a strange picture of a circle with an Indian chief in the center came on. I guess that my face showed that I wasn't impressed so Pat said, "Just wait until a show comes on, then you'll like it. We got your nickname from a little fairy named Tinkerbell on the Walt Disney Show. Now you can see who she is."

"My nickname's not Tinkerbell," I laughed.

"Well, we called you that as a baby. Then we shortened it to Tink," explained Pat.

I thought about this while I ate my bowl of porridge with brown sugar and canned milk and then went outside to play. I went next door to see if Darren Maxwell could play. He was the same age as me and had an older brother named Harry. They had lots of dinky toy cars. We would make towns with roads in the backyard dirt and play for hours or we would play marbles. Not today though because there was no one home.

Next, I went to see if I could visit Mr. Evan who lived next door to us. He was usually in the garage and would stop to talk to me for a while. Sometimes showing me tricks like how he could rub a penny in his hands and it would disappear! He was missing half a finger on one of his hands and he kept hoping that it would grow back. The garage door was shut so he was still in the house. Mrs. Evan didn't like me to knock, so I went across the street to the Martin's.

Mr. Martin was in the garden, as he always was, so I told him that we got a Television.

"You're full of prunes," he answered. He always said this to me, even though I didn't eat prunes. "You go see Mrs. Martin. I think she's got a muffin for you."

I went around to the kitchen door, got a big hug and a yellow muffin from Mrs. Martin. My Mum always knew where I was because Cocoa was with me. Whichever house I was visiting, he would be laying on the doorstep patiently waiting for me.

Today he stayed at the Martin's house until there was such a commotion outside that we both had to go see what was happening.

Next to Darren's yard, was a huge forest. I wasn't allowed to play in it because I could get lost. There was a gigantic, double tree, which was taller than any of the other trees in that forest. The tree started as one tree trunk and, about 20 feet up, it separated into two trunks or whole trees. It magnificently stood at the top end of our road.

Whenever the kids didn't really want you to do something, like play with them, they would dare you to climb the double tree. Of course, you wouldn't climb that huge tree, so then you couldn't play with them. Only today, someone took the dare, Amanda! She always wanted to hang around with Pat and his friends but they didn't want a dumb kid sister tagging along. So, they said she could hang around them, when she climbed the double tree. They never thought she would, but she did! The commotion was that she had climbed all 150 feet to the top and now was frozen with fear and could not move to climb back down. Pat and Mr. McGregor, from down the road, had climbed as far up as they could. To no avail, they were trying to talk her down. Then they called the fire truck! It was now screaming up the street with sirens blaring.

My poor Mum was, very shakily, standing in front of the Maxwell's house, looking so gray and tired. She had become accustomed to injuries with Scott, who was a bit of a dare devil and had already had several broken arms and a broken leg, but not so with Amanda.

Two of the firemen took ropes and began the climb telling Mr. McGregor and Pat to climb down first. Amanda was sobbing uncontrollably. She was holding on to the trunk so tightly that her hands were going numb. To make matters worse, she was so near the top of the tree that the trunk was almost as thin as a branch. The men couldn't go that far. The highest fireman had to stop about 3 feet below her and talk her into moving her hands just a little bit lower. Then she could move her foot down to the next branch 3 inches lower. This took at least 30 minutes, which felt like the longest time. Then, as Amanda began to trust the fireman a little more, she would move a little faster. Finally, she was within his reach! He could put a harness on her, that attached her to him, and they could climb down together!

Amanda was exhausted after this traumatic experience and, although Mum hugged her with pure relief, she knew that there would be consequences to pay after she got to sleep for a few hours. It was all worth it to her though. She had finally proven to those boys that she wasn't a chicken and was someone they would be proud to have in their group. Also, she had seen our neighborhood from a different perspective. It no longer appeared so big. She had seen it as a tiny part of the whole picture, like the little town in the department store window at Christmas. Now she realized that it no longer could contain her. She was bigger than it and would someday be free of its bonds!

Chapter 3

I was awakened by screams in the night. At first, I thought they were just the fire trucks in my dreams, but then there were loud men's voices and I knew this was not a dream. Pat and Amanda were standing in our upstairs bedroom window looking down.

"What's going on?" I asked.

This was one of those times that they wisely chose not to answer me. Only years later did I find out that Darren's Dad and his friend, after having several drinks, had gotten into a discussion about which man's wife had the bigger breasts. Then they decided to prove it. Much to the screaming and fighting women's disapproval, the men had torn off their blouses and bras and then pinned the women on their backs out on the front lawn! My oldest siblings shielded me from learning too early that some people could be so disgustingly cruel. I was just told that it was something that I didn't need to worry about, and to go back to sleep. When I saw Mrs. Maxwell's black eye and split lip the next day, I knew that her injury had something to do with what I didn't need to worry about. Today I wouldn't play with Darren or Harry.

Maybe Cathy Smith, who was only two, could have a visitor. She lived three houses down the road from us, and had a much older brother who was usually in trouble with his Dad. I wondered if he was really bad or if his Dad was like mine, so ashamed of himself that he took it out on his son. Darryl suffered so much abuse from his father that it seemed to have affected his mental capacity. I was afraid of him and would go home if he was there. Fortunately, he was not home, so I could stay for a visit. Cathy was the only person I knew who was younger than me, so I could make the rules for a change. We would play house and I could be the kind of Mum that I dreamed of. The type my Mum wished she could be, but her

9

circumstances did not allow. We would go shopping and I would bake cookies and cakes like on the family TV show. We played for hours until Corinne came to get me for dinner.

We had a nice dinner, my favorite, baked macaroni and cheese casserole. Mum could do wonders with just skim milk powder, macaroni noodles, some cracker crumbs and one cup of grated cheddar cheese! It was a nutritious, tasty, dinner that suited the budget.

It was almost the end of summer and almost time for the kids to go back to school. I wouldn't be going to kindergarten until next year because I had just turned 4 and you had to be 5. Corinne really liked to play school now, so that's what we did after supper. She made playing the most fun. She would set up wooden, Japanese orange boxes or upside-down buckets as seats for teddy bears and dolls. Then bigger boxes, or stacked up boxes, to be the desks. This way Corinne could be the teacher and there would be more kids in the class besides just me.

We didn't have extra paper to write on so we would use some of our storybooks. In the years to come, when we chose to sell the books, we found they could have been worth a fair bit of money but the printing we had done on the pages made them worthless. The memories of those happy schoolrooms meant more to me than the money anyways. Corinne would read me the stories as she read to the class.

The next day, when I was playing outside, a lady and her boy came to talk to my Mum. The boy was pushing a beautiful tricycle. It had pretty white wheels and a brown plastic seat that looked like a waffle iron, all smooth but with deep cut squares in it. I asked him why he wasn't riding it and he said. "It's too small for me. My new one is at home."

He played catch with me while our Mums had tea together. I kept missing the ball, but he waited patiently while I searched for it under the peonies. I heard the front door open and thought I was in trouble for rooting around in my Mum's plants! Instead, I got a nice surprise. My Mum introduced me to Mrs. White and Todd. She said, "They heard that you didn't have a tricycle. Todd has outgrown this one and they have decided to give it to you. Isn't that nice?"

"Wow my own bike?" escaped from my lips. I was so astonished! How could anyone just give away a bike? They didn't even know me. Wow. They must be rich! They lived down the street and around the corner. It was a place where I had never been before. I hope that I said, "Thank-you." Getting a bike from these people meant so much to me, more than I knew how to express. I hope they could tell by the awe-struck look on my face.

For the next three or four days, all I did was ride on and talk about my new bike! Late at night, after all us kids had gone to bed, I would sneak downstairs to tell Pat all about my bike. He was watching one of his favorite TV shows and he didn't even mind my interrupting. I think it brought him joy to see my excitement over my tricycle.

The next morning Corinne and I had to have a bath and get dressed up to go to a birthday party. I remembered Corinne's 7th and my 4th, birthday parties. We had played some fun games like "Farmer in the Dell" and "London Bridges" and had birthday cake, but we didn't have to wear dresses. I didn't even own a dress, so I had to wear one of Corinne's that was getting a little too small for her. Now it would be my dress! Corinne had a couple of other dresses, as she needed them for school. Two that used to be Amanda's and one that Mrs. Smith had bought for Corinne. That was before Mrs. Smith had a daughter of her own.

It felt so different to be walking down our street wearing a dress. Was everyone really looking at us or did I just feel that they were? Even the air felt different as it touched my little pudgy knees. We walked all the way to the bottom of our road where the store was and then we turned and walked passed to where I had never been before. We were beside the golf course that I had heard Pat, Amanda, and Scott talking about. It seemed almost mystical to see these places. I didn't realize how far we had gone when we arrived at a house and were knocking on the door. A very nice-looking lady, in a crisply pressed, orange, cotton dress with her hair all done up in a yellow, sequined covered bow, opened the door. Then I heard Amanda say, "Hello, this is Corinne and Hanna. I will be back to pick them up at 4 o'clock." As Amanda turned to leave the lady asked, "Would you like to stay, Amanda? You would be more than welcome." Flattered, Amanda said "Thank-you for the offer, but I have some chores at home that I must do."

I didn't even know the birthday girl. She was in Corinne's class and she had a little sister. So, when they heard that Corinne had a little sister, they asked me to come. As Amanda was leaving, many more prancing feet came running to greet us. Girls, about Corinne's size, in an assortment of colored dresses. Silk ribbons in their pony or pig tailed hair-does. The sight

11

that caught my eyes the most were their shoes. They were so beautiful. All black, smooth and shiny enough to see a reflection in. With tiny, thin straps and buckles!

"You go ahead to the backyard girls. We'll start some games in a few minutes." said the lady, as they rushed, giggling and jumping with Corinne. I followed, a little unsure. The backyard was amazing! It even had a playhouse in the corner! There was a play stove, sink and a little table with chairs. We took turns setting the tiny china teacups, sugar bowl, creamer and teapot out for afternoon tea. There were dolls with clothing and a crib! I would have played here forever but they were starting "London Bridges". Then we played a game that was new to me, "Pin the tail on the donkey". Next, we were called into the house to play "Musical chairs" in the basement. I was so hot and thirsty that I was glad when the lady said, "Let's go upstairs for something to eat and drink."

It was beautiful upstairs! There were pink and yellow balloons hanging from little ribbons all over the ceiling! The table was set with a beautiful paper tablecloth with Cinderella all over it, paper plates, napkins and cups to match! After we were all shown to our seats the lady brought in plates of sandwiches with no crusts! I don't know where they got bread that didn't have crusts but I wish we could get it. There were peanut butter and jam sandwiches, egg sandwiches and some really special circle ones of peanut butter with a banana in the middle! We could have red Kool-Aid, orange Kool-Aid or milk. I knew that Mum didn't like us to have Kool-Aid but I hoped she wouldn't mind just for today.

Then it was time for cake! It was so beautiful with candles and smarties all over it! We had to wait until everyone had a piece before we could start eating it and the wait was excruciating! It was so good. White cake with sweet frosting and the biggest surprise of all…MONEY in it! I put a forkful of cake in my mouth and found a shiny silver coin with a picture of a sailboat on one side and the Queen's head on the other.

It was at this party that I realized all people didn't live the same way. I was so astounded by this party that I actually felt dizzy. Then the lady brought out a tray covered with tiny, smooth, pink plastic baskets filled with candies. She gave each of us one. There were little multi-colored candies that I hadn't seen before, jelly beans and even a jeweled ring! Some of the girls were running around now and some were going home. I was just so happy to sit and look at the beautiful candies and my "dime" as Corinne called it. The lady said, "Hanna, your sister's here," and I looked up to see Amanda at the door. The time had gone so fast!

"Could I take some of these candies home to share with my brothers and sisters," I asked the lady.

"Of course, those are yours and you can do whatever you would like with them," she answered.

I poured as many candies out of the basket as I thought my hand could hold.

"Oh darling, you can take the basket too. It's for you," chuckled the lady.

Corinne looked pretty embarrassed by me. I guess I shouldn't have tried to take so many candies, but I wanted some for Pat, Amanda, Scott and Mum.

On the walk home, I chattered like a little squirrel. There was so much to tell Amanda about. Corinne mentioned a few things. I guess it wasn't quite as exciting to her because she had been to other parties. We walked back by crossing the road and going along the railroad tracks. This ran behind some backyards, and was a lot quieter at this time of day than the busy road. We could see in people's yards and I was really surprised when I saw that someone had a tricycle just like mine.

"Look Amanda," I shouted, "that bike's the same as mine!"

A big man dressed in blue jeans and a T shirt with rolled up sleeves was crossing the yard to the tricycle and shouted, "Hey you kids, get away from my fence!"

We weren't near his fence, but still our pace quickened and no one spoke until we were well away from there.

"Do you think that was actually Tink's bike," Corinne asked Amanda? "It really looks just like it." I sure hoped they were wrong!

We walked by the lot we called "the land of fairies." We called it that because it was filled with thistles that released those white fluffy seed pods. We would try to catch them and make wishes. I tried to catch as many as I could, so I could wish my tricycle safe at home. We all ran up our hill when we reached our street, hoping to be the first to spot my bike. Of course, being the youngest I was the last one there and I could tell by the long looks on their faces that my bike was gone. I didn't want to, because I knew that it would make everyone else sad, but I couldn't help but start

13

crying. I sobbed so hard that I fell to the grass and felt that I could not breathe. My poor bike, it would be so afraid. I really believed, at this age, that everything had feelings.

Corinne still tells people, 40 years later, how I used to cover my ornaments with Kleenex as blankets at night so they wouldn't get cold. It wasn't until I was in my thirties that I could understand why I took such good care of those inanimate objects. When I was little, I had seen so many people treated badly by others, as though they didn't know that those people had feelings. I was afraid maybe the ornaments had feelings too and we just didn't know it. I didn't want them to suffer the same way as those misunderstood people.

Scott didn't even wait for Pat to get home to tell him about my bike. Instead, he rode his bike to find Pat on his paper route. They agreed to finish the route together so Pat could be home earlier.

I was playing cut-out dolls on my bed when Pat came in and, sitting down on the edge of my bed said," Oh Tink, what are we going to do about your bike?"

"A bad man took it, and it's in his yard. Do you think we can sneak in and get it back?" I pleaded.

"Then we would be the bad people," said Pat. "It might just be better if we go talk to the man. Maybe he doesn't know that it's your bike?"

Before we even had dinner Pat and I went to talk to the man. "Are you sure that this is the house?" asked Pat.

I nodded my head in reply. After taking a deep breath, he knocked on the door. We waited and no one answered, but we could hear that the television was on. So, Pat knocked a little louder and we waited again. The doorknob turned and the man I had seen earlier opened the door. He was still dressed the same and was holding a can of beer. "Good evening Sir." said Pat, "My little sister thinks she saw her tricycle in your backyard."

"Are you accusing me of stealing her bike?" shouted the man.

"No Sir, by no means. It is possible that a child may have borrowed it and rode it into your yard," Pat calmly replied. "So now you're accusing my kid of stealing?!" the man retorted.

"Please try to understand, Sir. We couldn't afford to buy my sister a bike and some kind people gave her one, so all we're trying to do is get it back." my brother replied out of exasperation.

"Well maybe you stole it in the first place and it wasn't really a gift! Now I get it. You better get the hell off my property you bloody thief before I teach you a lesson." slurred the man, spitting and spraying as he spoke. Pat grabbed my hand and I was away from the house before I knew what was happening. He was running with me in tow and I looked back to see the man in his front yard, wielding a baseball bat and cursing at us.

I was very sad the next morning. Not just because I had lost my bike, but also because I knew Pat felt sad for not getting it back from the man. I tagged around with Pat all morning hoping that I could do something to cheer him up.

"Tink, I have to go mow Mr. Robert's lawn now so I'll see you later," stammered Pat.

My staying with him had done nothing to ease his mind of the responsibility.

 Chapter 4

I spent the rest of the day visiting my neighbors. Cocoa was following as always but now our cat Buttons and her 6 kittens were following as well! My Mum always wished that she had had a camera then to catch the image of that parade.

I remember the day I found out how cats have their kittens. We all knew that Buttons had kittens in her tummy but no one would tell me how she was going to get them out. I just happened to go into the little shed by our kitchen door, to get something for Mum, when I saw it. In the shed, there was a tall cupboard style cabinet. Inside it, there were already a bunch of kittens out of Buttons's tummy. As I opened the door, I saw Buttons on the floor with another one in her mouth. I was so proud! I ran back into the house shouting, "I know how cats have kittens!"

"Oh, you do, do you? How then?" asked Pat.

"They cough them up!" I announced. It made sense to me!

The next morning was hectic for Mum as it was the first day of school. She needed to make sure all the kids were fed, clean, dressed and had their school supplies and milk money in bags to take with them. I watched the excitement and, as the last one shut the back door behind them, there was a knock on the front door. I knew that I wasn't to open the door to strangers so I waited for my Mum to get it. When she did, there was a man saying that he was there to take our TV.

"No, you can't have it." my Mum said as she shut the door. "That man (meaning our father) never pays for anything when he should, but he promised to pay for this, for the kids. You'll have to go after him for the money!"

I was relieved to see that Darren was outside. I wanted to get away from my Mum and this man fighting over the television. Darren also didn't have to go to school this year as he wouldn't turn 5 until next year. I went outside to join him. Before I knew it, Mum was calling me in for lunch. After I ate my peanut butter and jam sandwich, I took my marbles, 2 clear glass ones with colored ribbons inside, and I went back outside. Darren and I played with our marbles for the whole afternoon. Sometimes we would play the game the kids taught us but mostly we would just do our own games of rolling them and lining them up. Soon Corinne came home and changed from her school clothes into her play clothes. She didn't really like school yet, when she got home, she would always want to play it. Scott was home next, changed and off to his friend David's house. Amanda and Pat would be a little longer yet as they were in High School. They got out later and it was further to walk.

When Pat got home, he said he had found a surprise for me while he was walking. He held out a silver metal thing, that was all shiny, with a chain in the middle, a big circle on one end and a broken circle on the other end. "Do you know what these are?" he asked.

I had never seen anything like it before. I just shook my head, no.

"These are handcuffs, like the police use," he explained. "They use them to hold a bad guy's hands together so he won't fight. One hand goes in this circle and the other hand goes in here. You see these two sides click together, around his arm, and make a circle like this side."

"Can we put them together," I asked?

"You can decide that, because it's yours now. We don't have the key to open it again, so you mustn't put it around anyone's wrist or you'll never get it off, once you close it, it will be closed forever," was Pat's answer.

This was a hard decision for me, I thought about it very carefully. Something "forever" was special and Pat would want me to be careful. The process was so painful to me that my decision was to do it now, so I wouldn't have to think about it anymore. I felt the occasion was so special because Pat had trusted me to make the decision. I didn't know then what a big part of Pat's life handcuffs would be.

It soon seemed like the family was back to routine, with school back in. As if our lives could be called routine? My days were whiled away in a mystical, 4-year old's haze. Making mud pies, carefully decorated with the yellow petals of broom, and stuck meticulously to the white siding walls of the south side of our house to dry in the sun. I could leave them there for hours and come back to find them hardened just right when they dropped off the house into little hard bricks. My Mum didn't appreciate my endeavors, and told me not to do this anymore! I was very hurt and couldn't understand why she was so angry?

"Why so glum, chum?" wondered Pat, who was just returning from school to start his paper route.

My emotions were so confused and Pat's caring interest was just the ticket to bring instant tears to my eyes. After several huffing moments of explanation, I had told my story. Pat took my hand in his, walked me to that white wall that was now covered with gray circles and he said, "This is why Mum doesn't want you to do that anymore."

I felt so much better. She did like my mud pies. She just didn't like the mess they left on her wall!

Darren, Harry and I would spend hours pretending we were Roy Rogers and Dale Evans. Darren was always Roy and I was Dale and Harry would be the bad guy who usually tied me up. This was fun except sometimes they would forget about me and I would remain captive until somebody's Mum would come and untie me! Some days we would go down to the field of fairies, pick them, then blow and make wishes. We were always careful to be on the lookout for the man in the neighborhood who had stolen my bike.

Chapter 5

The trees were losing their leaves now, forcing Pat to rake them into piles and stack them in the compost box. I thought they were so special and I loved to roll in the piles until Pat gave me a rake to help clean them up and get them into the box. Pat would also rake some of the neighbor's leaves to earn his own money and soon Scott was doing the same.

One day Corinne came home from school saying that she felt really hot and wanted to go to bed. This certainly was a sign for Mum, as Corinne often would say she felt sick before school but not after! Mum gently laid her hand on Corinne's forehead and said with a slight frown, "Yes, you really do have a fever. I'll give you two children's aspirin with some water and get you into bed."

Corinne's fever persisted the next day and the day after. Mum had called the doctor and he would be by that afternoon, after office hours, to see what the problem was. Usually, when Corinne was home from school, we could play some games on her bed. This time, because Mum didn't know what was wrong with Corinne, she didn't want me to get too close. The doctor came by that afternoon with his stethoscope and all! He said, "It's a little hard to tell at this point just what it is. There are several childhood maladies going around in the schools right now and in a day or two we'll know which one it is. Until then just keep her on aspirin, plenty of fluids, and bed rest. Let me know if any rashes or discomfort appear."

Again, that night I slept with Amanda in her double bed. The next morning Corinne awoke covered in spots and the Dr. verified it to be measles. He instructed Mum that we were all to stay indoors now until the disease had run its course. All of us children would have been susceptible. The Dr. would be sending the quarantine officer by today to post the sign on our door. It would have to stay up until the last child's spots had been there for five days. The incubation period was 10 days to onset of fever, 13 to 15 days to appearance of spots or rash. This meant we would all be cooped up in our house for two weeks or more!

Mum hardly had time to call the schools to tell them we would be absent for quite a duration, when we heard hammering on the front door! "Quarantined", in big letters then, in smaller print, it read, "These premises contain an infectious disease. Do not enter!" A moment later, tapping on the back door meant another sign going up. I felt humiliated when people walked by and saw our sign. It was also frightening when Mum realized she couldn't go out to get more aspirin or groceries! She hoped that our Dad would be home in time to get these things. She checked the aspirins and, seeing there was only one dose left, she knew she had to come up with another plan. She called our Auntie Bernice. Explaining the whole situation, she asked if they could drop by with some aspirin. Aunt Bernice agreed instantly and explained that our Uncle Sigmond would drop it by our back door as soon as he was off work at 5 o'clock. She was true to her word. At 5:45 we heard the car coming down our driveway. We heard the engine switch off, the door open, a rustling of bags and a few heavy steps on the porch. Then Uncle Sigmond's voice yelled, "I'll just set these things down here. You can get them when I'm gone. You take care of yourselves. Bernice and I will be praying for you and if you need anything else, don't hesitate to call." Mum shouted back, "Thank you so much Sigmond. I don't know what we would have done without the children's medicine!"

When he was gone, Pat opened the door to get the aspirins. There on the porch were three large brown grocery bags! A note on top explained, "I knew that you would also need some essentials as well as aspirin. It was the least that we could do! Please just take care of the kids and yourself. Bernice." There was a 10lb. bag of flour, two dozen eggs, a gallon of milk, 5 lbs. Quaker oats, a bag with 10 apples, plus three boxes of children's aspirin.

Six days later I started the fever followed within a day or two by Scott, Amanda, and then Pat. It was an exhausting time for our Mother, trying to keep us all served with water, aspirin, cool cloths for our heads and the little food we felt like eating. I can remember how weak I felt with the fever and how itchy the spots were. The worst, most frightening thing that happened was when my eye started jumping and I screamed, "I'm getting a measle in my eye!" I was completely terrified, thinking I may be blind if the bump came up in my eye!

Mum came running, "What's going on?"

I repeated, "I'm getting a measle in my eye!"

"You can't get a measle in your eye," Mum reassured me, taking my hands down from over my eyes. Seeing the lid of my eye twitch, she tried not to laugh as she explained that I just had a nerve jumping in my eyelid. She gave me a face cloth to hold over it until it stopped jumping. She told me it was just scared and would stop as soon as it felt safe.

Finally, 20 days later, the man returned to remove our signs and life returned to normal.

Chapter 6

In the winter, Pat and Scott shoveled snow to make money. We loved the snow most of all since we could build snowmen, snow forts and throw snowballs! When we got too cold to stay out anymore we would go inside for warm milk with honey in it. This is when I learned about Christmas. My brothers and sisters told me all about the baby Jesus and how he had no clothes or a house to live in. This made me realize how lucky I was! Then they told me about Santa Claus, the amazingly generous, loving man who cared so much for children. I started dreaming of what I would ask Santa for when I went to see him. I felt that I was floating on a cloud dreaming of these wonderful possibilities.

Several days of searching in the department store catalogue for the perfect toy passed quickly. That evening when Mum tucked me into bed she said, "Tomorrow I will take you and Corinne down to the department store so you can see their beautiful Christmas window and sit on Santa's lap."

I thought I would not be able to sleep with "thoughts of sugarplums dancing in my head," and then I awoke to morning! We had bowls filled with warm oatmeal, topped with brown sugar and canned milk, enough to hold us through until we returned home from town. We got dressed in school clothes, matching wool plaid skirts with leotards and sweaters. It was a cold, snowy day and we would be walking to the bus stops and waiting for buses, so we needed to be warm and had to look nice for Santa!

I was so excited to be going to see Santa that I hadn't even thought about the bus! I had never been on a bus before! This was a great day! Waiting for the bus, with my Mum and Corinne, felt so special. I stood so proudly and then the bus stopped for us. The metal door swung open to reveal stairs! I had never imagined stairs in a bus before but I managed quite easily to straddle up the steps with my little two feet tall legs, not knowing that one day I would be envious of this.

The bus continued on its route to downtown carrying one wide-eyed, amazed little girl and her much embarrassed, older sister. She was embarrassed because I was singing, "The wheels on the bus go round and round". I had to do something with the excitement that was sure to suffocate me otherwise!

It felt like just minutes we had been on the bus when my Mum said, "Would you like to pull the buzzer to let the bus driver know that we want to get off?" pointing to the cable for me to pull. It was even easier to go down those bus stairs than it had been to climb in. We were standing on a sidewalk, which turned out to be right in front of the department store. There was a wall of people crowded around what Mum said was the window that we wanted to see. We stood patiently, my nose almost pressed right into a boy's smelly wool coat. We had to keep moving ahead if we wanted to see the "Christmas magic" as my Mum called it. Finally, the boy with the smelly wool coat stepped behind me and my eyes were bedazzled by twinkling, colored lights, drifting snow and the happiest little village there could ever be. The little houses looked so cozy and warm, the little figurines so happy, either carrying home packages or skating on the frozen pond in the park. You could hear the Christmas carols the people were singing. I imagined myself and my whole family, into that little world.

"Can we go inside to see Santa now girls? It is getting very cold out here." My Mum's old winter coat had worn so thin that there would not be much warmth left in it.

I felt very frightened to go and see Santa but I trusted Corinne, and if she was brave enough to go, then it must be okay.

We walked into the store. It was so nice and warm, with beautiful red and green ribbons all tied around the big pillars. Christmas carols were playing and everyone was wishing us a "Merry Christmas". I felt that I was imaging us still in the tiny village. We had to go out the back door of the store to get to Santa's workshop. The most beautiful, snow covered cabin was just outside the door! Suddenly my legs were shaking and I felt like throwing up. A few tears slipped down my cheek but I knew that Corinne would be so ashamed of me if I started to cry. Instead I bit my lower lip, grasped Corinne's hand and started walking toward what I felt was certain death!

"Ho-Ho-Ho, Merry Christmas!" laughed a friendly voice. "Who will be next to climb upon my knee to tell me their Christmas wishes?" "Us" said a timid little voice that I was surprised to see came from Corinne. I learned from that moment on to have the greatest respect for my older sister Corinne. She was not much bigger than I, nor was she really much braver than I, but she was strong enough from within to stand up for what she believed in and to do what she felt was needed. Holding my hand, she led me up the red, carpet stairs to Santa's big soft armchair. Here we stopped until Santa, who was not a powerful beast, but just a jolly, happy, Grandpa type man said, "Jump up here, honey," gesturing to his knee. "I'll help you up here Sweetie," he said as he bent down and picked me up too.

This was such a magical day, was this really happening? My whole body tingled with excitement!

"Now what would you like Santa to leave under your Christmas tree?" he asked.

Corinne spoke very quietly, "Could I please have a pretty pink dress with short sleeves and ruffles?" I was speechless. Could I really ask for anything? My mind was a whirl with all the pictures from the catalogue dancing in my head!

"What about you little girl, would you like a dolly?" suggested Santa, helping me out with an idea.

"Yes, please," was all I could muster.

"Well, you both behave and we'll see what Santa can do on Christmas Eve. For now, I'll give you each a candy cane and a china bell to decorate your Christmas tree with. Merry Christmas Ho-Ho-Ho!" he bellowed.

The bus ride home was filled with our endless chatter about all the exciting things that we had seen today! We were so blissfully happy. Somehow, it had even made a change in our Mother. It was like a long, closed window had opened and a younger, more vibrant, woman had emerged.

Days passed quickly with fragrant scents of Christmas baking, sounds of carols being sung, and laughter bubbling over. It was so special to be surrounded by loving brothers, sisters and my Mum.

One day we went in to the forest to choose the perfect tree. After cutting it down and taking it home, we enjoyed several happy hours making paper chains to wrap around it. We then carefully chose where to hang our few glass balls and our treasured china bells. We felt there could be no tree more beautiful than ours.

While sitting closely together, gazing at our tree, there seemed to be a blanket of serenity enveloping us. Then our Mother spoke slowly in a trembling voice, "I know that you all know the story of how Santa goes all around the world every Christmas Eve to bring joy and toys to all children." She paused to look at each of us individually as her eyes began to fill with tears. "There are so many children, that each year Santa must choose some children to miss and I am afraid he said that this is your year." The air was suddenly very cold, as if the blanket had been ripped away. No one spoke. There was no sound. I felt that maybe they were all holding their breath, as I realized that I was. Then Pat said, "What matters most is that we will all be together!"

I don't remember being too affected by this disappointment, as I think that I was too young. I couldn't remember last Christmas so I didn't really understand what I had lost. It must have been very difficult for Corinne, who was right at the age of wonderment with the magic of Christmas. Scott always managed to appear to be okay, but I think it was only his survivor training that had taught him this. For Pat and Amanda, I think it was a heavy burden that left an insatiable hole in their souls. They, like our Mother, felt the terrible loss for "our" childhood, not the loss for themselves. For me, Pat had said the only words that really mattered, "We would all still be together!" The rest of the evening passed very quietly and I think all of our pillows silently soaked away our unspoken feelings that night.

A few days later Pat walked me down to the Naval base, where our Dad worked. "This will be a lot of fun for you, Tink!" he explained "You have to be under 7 years old to attend, that's why Corinne went to a different Christmas party with Scott. You get to go on the ship for a ride around the harbor, to see Santa and have lunch. Then I'll come back to get you after you have all that fun!"

I really didn't want to go if Pat didn't go with me but I felt he wouldn't be happy with me if I told him that. Sometimes we just have to be brave and do what we're told! He seemed so excited for me, I didn't want to ruin it.

Turning the next corner, we were in full view of the ship. Streamers were hanging all over it and men were jumping down from gangplanks, with arms outstretched to gather up arriving children.

"Here we are, doesn't this look like fun? Give me a hug, have a good time and I'll be here when you get back." Pat assured me, just as I was scooped up into the arms of a smiling, welcoming sailor. "I bet you'd like to have some lunch? What do you like best peanut butter sandwiches or liver and onions?"

"Don't be silly, Fred. Little girls don't like liver and onions," chuckled a colorful clown. He rubbed my nose with his big red rubber one. "You can have whatever you like, peanut butter, cheese or egg sandwiches, or hot dogs or macaroni."

They had carried me into the ship while they were talking.

"We are now in what we call the mess. This is where we eat, so you just have to tell us what you want," he continued. I had never had so many men hovering around me and, I have to say, I liked all of the attention. Then after I had finished my bowl of macaroni and a glass of chocolate milk one sailor asked me, "Who's your daddy, honey?"

"Chad Rutherford," I answered. Even at four a child knows when they have said something wrong. Just that second of pause in his down turned eyes, I knew it meant something.

"Ho-Ho-Ho Merry Christmas!" Jingle bells were ringing and Santa appeared in the room! He handed his overflowing sack to one of the men saying, "Would you boys help old Santa out with giving away these toys to the right girl and boys, because I can't stay too long. I have so much to do and Christmas is almost here! Ho-Ho-Ho!" Then he strolled up and down the aisles of tables giving out candy canes. Soon he was gone.

The sailors were passing out the presents from Santa's bag and they handed me one. I was very afraid. Was this a test or something? I was terrified that something really bad would happen to me if I took that present. I started to cry.

"What's the matter, Sugar? Did you think they missed giving you a present?" asked a sailor.

The ominous feeling surrounding me made it hard to breathe, as if it were squeezing the life out of me. Solemnly I answered, "My Mum explained that we're not supposed to get presents this year as it's our turn for Santa to miss us." I don't know how they could understand what I said as my sobbing was taking my words away with the hiccups.

What seemed like ages passed and then a man said, "Oh, Sweetie, you don't need to worry. We have special connections with Santa and you never know what good things can happen. This present is for you. Open it up so we all can see."

I felt very embarrassed with those people watching me but the package was open in an instant. Inside there was the most beautiful doll I had ever seen! She was about 8" tall with straight black hair and brown eyes that shut when you laid her down. She wore a blue and white dress and a beige coat with a fur collar. "She looks just like you and she has real hair," said a sailor.

As an adult, looking back, I know he was teasing me then because the hair was so fake but, at that age, I believed that it grew on her head!

Then another sailor said, "It's time to pack her up so you can take her home. It's time to go."

The party had been so exciting that I was feeling a little dizzy and disoriented as I clutched my doll to make sure that she was real.

"Let me carry you up the gang plank little lady. We don't want to lose you overboard this close to Christmas." No sooner had the sailor spoken, that I was lifted to his chest and whisked away into the fading light of the late afternoon. Pat was there at the ropeway and I was so excited to show him my doll.

The long walk home was amplified by my eagerness to share with my family all that I had seen and done. It seemed like days to me that Pat and I trudged on, but at last we were home!

Everyone took a turn to hold and examine my doll. Even Cocoa had to have a sniff. Corinne had gotten a Snakes and Ladder's game and Scott had a car model from the older children's party that they attended. The air of excitement was almost palpable but I lay in my bed that night wishing something good would happen for Pat, Amanda and Mum as well.

The next day passed so quickly as I took my new doll around for everyone I knew to see. My neighbors all asked about my trip on the boat and what I had for lunch. I felt so lucky to have something so special to tell them all. That was the first night I dreamt a horrible dream that would haunt me for the next several months. In the distance, I would see a pink florescent ball that was rolling towards me. It would grow larger and larger as it continued to get closer and I would always awake crying just as it was about to crush me.

I awoke to morning and Christmas just 2 sleeps away. I ran downstairs to see our beautiful tree. Something looked different about it? Then I realized my china bell was missing and the big glass ball with the colored stripes wasn't there either.

"Yah, Tink you noticed too? The cat climbed the tree and knocked it over, so some things got broken." apologized Pat. I could not answer because I was so upset about my china bell that Santa gave me. When Pat went back into the kitchen I just turned and went back upstairs to my room to cry. Corinne came in and put her arm around me saying, "It's so unfair. Poor Buttons gets blamed when it was really our father's fault. He came home drunk again, stumbled and fell into the tree. He knocked it over!"

As if on cue, the doorbell rang and we could hear people singing Christmas carols. Corinne and I ran to the top of the stairs just in time to see Pat open the door. There was a group of men outside who began carrying in boxes filled with things! We froze to watch in amazement as the boxes just kept coming!

One of the men had put his box down in our kitchen and was walking to go back out the front door when he spotted Corinne and I at the top of the stairs. "I hope you little ladies are behaving so Santa will be by to see you soon" he said. Then I recognized him as the sailor who told me that my doll had real hair! I was so surprised! "Hi", was all I could say! "How did you know where my house is?" escaped from my lips. "Christmas is full of all kinds of surprises," he answered, "Bye, bye for now" and he waved as he walked out the door.

The second the door shut, Corinne and I were on our feet running down the stairs to see what all those boxes were about. In the living room, there were three boxes on the couch. And, there were some stacked on the floor by the kitchen door. Boxes were also stacked on the kitchen counter and table! We were so excited, until we saw our Mum sitting on a kitchen chair crying. Suddenly we felt sick. How could we have misunderstood that this was a good thing when it made our Mum so unhappy? I know I felt the air had suddenly gone sour and unbreathable. "What's the matter, Mummy?" asked Corinne, in almost a whisper, as if she was afraid to hear the answer. With a chuckle Mum said, "Things couldn't be better! These are tears of happiness at our good fortune! Those men brought us all the food we need for a wonderful Christmas dinner. Turkey, potatoes, brussel sprouts, carrots, Xmas pudding and even cranberry sauce. Also, we have enough food for the month. A sack of flour, eggs, milk and fruit. You run upstairs and play while Amanda, Pat and I put these away."

We left the kitchen as quickly as possible, so not to pop the bubble of magic that was surrounding us. Corinne and I played Snakes and Ladders almost all day with my doll sitting beside us watching.

The next day was Christmas Eve. The day passed much as any other but the evening was filled with family closeness. There seemed to be something in the air. Maybe some secrets, but I wasn't worried about what they were. It was just so comforting to be with my family, singing Christmas carols and hearing stories about the first Christmas. Lastly, Pat read to us "Twas the Night Before Christmas". Then we all got one of Pat's big, gray work socks to put by our beds for our Christmas stocking. I really didn't understand what it was for but I was too tired to worry about it and was soon fast asleep.

"Wake up, Hanna. It's Christmas," Corinne said, "Look what's in your stocking."

My head was still fuzzy with sleep and I couldn't remember what a stocking was. Hearing a sort of jingle bell sound, I jumped to awareness! The sound came from Corinne's stocking. In it was a ring of five jingle bells brightly painted and tied with a ribbon to hang on the tree. On her bed, was an already opened package that had held a brush, comb, and mirror set. It was so pretty! "Hurry up and open your presents so we can eat our oranges together." She added.

I turned to see where my stocking had been left empty last night and sure enough there it was stuffed with something! I reached down inside of it and the first thing that my fingers touched was a hard sausage shaped present. I started peeling the tape off of the paper carefully so as not to tear it. "You don't do it like that!" Corinne said exasperated. The suspense was killing her and once again I was annoying her. "You probably think that the Santa's on the paper have feelings so you won't tear them!" I just wanted to save the paper because I never knew when I might need it. I think I knew too well how it felt not to have something when you needed it, so I wanted to be prepared. Eventually I had the paper off to discover a game of pickup sticks inside! Corinne waited while I opened the next present that was in my stocking. It was three new pairs of panties. Now Corinne and I could eat our Japanese oranges together. I had never had one before and I loved how easily they peeled! The little sections came apart so easily and they were just about the right size for our mouths. The sweet, cool juice was a real treat while we waited for the rest of our family to wake up. Or at least we tried to wait for them to awake.

Pat and Scott's room was right across the hall from ours, so we opened our door to see if they were awake. We couldn't hear any noise from their room at first but, while we played pickup sticks waiting for them, we heard Pat say, "All right you two, come on in!"

We burst into the room with all of our new things to show. Now we got to watch them open their stockings. Scott got what he called a whirly gig. It was a long plastic stick with helicopter blades. When you spun it between your two palms it would fly away. He also got underwear and a Japanese orange. Pat got three bottles of model paints, some underwear and an orange.

At this point, Pat said, "Well you guys wait while I go down and plug in the Christmas tree lights, then I'll call you to come down." The air was so full of excitement and I wasn't even sure why. We had seen the tree light up before but the anticipation was still there! Mum and Amanda's bedrooms were downstairs next to each other by the living room. We guessed that Pat was making sure they were awake too. Finally, we heard, "You guys can come down now." The three of us rushed down. I was last as always. The living room curtains were still closed, so the tree lights gave off such a nice glow along with the one prickly, snow sprayed, wreath with a Christmas light candle in the middle that hung in our front window. The few tree ornaments seemed like more in this light and there was something new under the tree. Presents! Mum and Amanda were sitting on a couch and chair in the living room, in their housecoats and slippers. Mum didn't really have slippers but she just wore our Dad's.

"Everyone find a seat now and Scott will hand out the presents." organized Pat.

The first gift was handed to Mum. We had all received gifts already, I was so happy to see that Mum got one too. She carefully opened the paper to find a pair of gloves and a scarf inside. With a tear in her eye she held it up to show us and she said, "Thank you Santa." So, he had come after all. I guess the sailors were right that sometimes really good things could happen. Then Scott brought another present over to Corinne. We all watched as she opened it. It was a paint by numbers of a farmland scene. The next gift was handed to Amanda. The paper, carefully pulled aside, revealed a soft pink shell with matching cardigan in faux angora wool. She dashed from the room, leaving a small squeal in the air behind her. Scott left a package on his chair next, saying, "I'll open it later." Then he brought a gift to Pat. Pat shook it, felt the paper more carefully, smelled it, and then announced, "I believe that it might be a pair of shoes." He began to open the package and he was correct. His old pair were wearing out, and were really too small for his feet, so he was especially pleased. Amanda returned from her bedroom donning her new sweater set, as Scott handed me a gaily wrapped gift. I began to undo the ribbons that held my surprise, when the paper slid away to reveal a coloring book and crayons. It was a bigger book than I had ever seen and it would fill many hours with peaceful memories. Now, 40 years later, I am still soothed by the smell of crayons! There was just one package remaining to be opened, the one Scott had left on his seat. He said that he had forgotten about it, but he always joked like that. We all watched him open a set of 4 screwdrivers, which he probably still has 40 years later. He would proudly show them to you so you could admire his thriftiness.

I don't think that I had ever seen my Mother as happy as she was this day! First there had been gifts for all of us, then there was enough food to keep her busy the rest of the day cooking us a marvelous Christmas dinner! We didn't know that she had been up before any of us. At 5AM she had been stuffing the 24lb turkey, to have it baking in the oven by 6 AM, to be ready to eat at 6 PM. Our father liked to eat at that time and, even though he seldom showed up to eat with us, she always held out hope that he would, especially for Christmas! We spent the day surrounded by the warmth of family, the oven cooking our fragrant bird. Because of the new snowfall, we also went out to play, until the cold had crept through our worn mittens.

The six of us were about half way through our delicious feast, having even said a blessing before the meal on Jesus' birthday, when a mixed blessing appeared! Our father arrived home to have dinner with his wife and 5 children! Everyone was so polite to each other, sharing all their stories from the day and passing all of the dinner delights. Anyone looking in at this festive scene would have thought of us as the ideal family. Some of us held onto this fantasy image, each of us for different reasons and for different lengths of time. Some maybe never letting go of this idea, even though our father's behavior continued to grow worse along with his drinking. As an adult, I now understand that Christmas that year would not have been so wonderful without the kindness of those sailors. They knew my Dad and understood what his wife and children must be going through at home. To this day, I still cherish that Christmas and make a point of donating to other families in need each year.

Chapter 7

My Dad's angry outbursts happened mostly at night while we younger children were asleep. He would accuse our Mother of such things as stealing his money and then he would strike out at her and anyone else who got in his way. Usually that was Pat. He would intervene for our Mother's sake.

Finally, in May of that year, things got so bad that Amanda and Pat decided to do what our Mother could not do herself. Move Dad out. Mum couldn't do it because of the love she still felt for him. They packed all of his personal belongings and put them outside. They could not afford to have the locks changed but they knew our Dad would not be able to find his keys when he got home drunk anyway. This gave our Mother the strength to apply for a divorce and to call the police the many times he came banging on the doors cursing and threatening us. The neighbors were awakened several times but similar occurrences happened at their homes as well. In fact, the one family on our street, that seemed to be the model family at that time, surprised us all years later when the father died and at the funeral it was discovered that he had a second wife and two children! He worked during the day as a bartender and was believed to work at nights driving a taxi. We baby boomers blamed the downfall of our families on the aftermath of the Second World War.

The next several months passed by in a blur. I never felt the turbulence of the divorce. Dad was never there even when he had lived with us. The custody proceedings went without incidence, as our father did not attend them. Although, our Mother had to relive every heart wrenching moment of her married life, to let the court see why she deserved a divorce and why she should have sole custody of the children. Soon both the marriage and the school year had ended and summer was upon us.

Now I was almost 5, I was allowed to go down the street to the store! Walking there with Corinne one morning, we found a treasure! Down one of the dirt banks near the sidewalk there was all this money. Corinne and I greedily scooped up every coin we saw. Afterwards, Corinne counted it and said there was $5.64 altogether. I didn't know the value of money but, somehow, I had managed to pick up more dimes and Corinne had more nickels. She was trying to trade with me saying that the nickels were worth more because they were bigger. I would not trade though, for fear of hurting the dimes' feelings. Sometimes my over caring paid off. The two of us rushed straight to the store to buy all of those candies we so often dreamed of.

Clutching our little bags of goodies, we rushed home to tell of our good fortune. I think that Corinne and I were still young enough to believe that some good fairies had put the money there for us but really it turned out that Amanda's boyfriend had spilled out his wallet last night by mistake, and could not see the coins in the dark. We could not take the candy back now, so we had to at least offer Trevor our candy. To our astonishment he said, "Don't worry about it. You just enjoy the candy."

My fifth birthday arrived in August of 1960! I was so excited because now I could go to kindergarten! I was just a little disappointed, though, as I thought that I would go tomorrow. I didn't understand that it didn't start until next month. At least there was the excitement of my birthday party! All of my friends came: Darren, Harry, Cathy and Corinne. Amanda, Scott and Pat were too old to want to play the childish games but Amanda helped to run them. We played all the favorites: London Bridges, Farmer in the Dell, Go-go-go-stop and Pin the Tail on the Donkey. Then we had my birthday cake and I got to open presents. Darren and Harry brought me a bag of new marbles. There were cat's eyes, steelies, crystals and many others. Cathy's Mum had sewn me a new skirt that I sure could use for school. It was so cute! It was pink, with a gathered waist, and little white kittens dancing around it. After the party, the kids just stayed and we played outside until dinnertime.

When they went home, I was playing alone on the front steps when my Dad's car pulled in our driveway. I was very surprised and scared because I had not seen him in a long time. I didn't know if his being here would cause a fight. He was already out of the car and standing on the porch. He was handing a present to me, "Happy Birthday, Tink." he said, with a twinkle in his eye. I didn't know if I was allowed to take a present from him now he was divorced from my Mum. "Go ahead and open it!" he urged me. It wasn't really wrapped in paper but was tied in a bag. I felt embarrassed for him that he didn't know how to wrap a gift. Inside was a tiny, grown up doll. "Her name is Debbie and when you get more clothes for her you can play with her just like you play with your cut outs," my Dad explained to me. Then I saw that the twinkle in his eye was really a tear. I had never seen him cry before and I was very sad. "What's the matter, Daddy?" I asked, not really wanting an answer. Then he really started to cry and hugged me in his arms saying, "You can't be my pretty little girl anymore!" I felt as if my heart was chocking me and I began to cry too. "Let me ask Mummy if you can come inside?" I managed to say thinking that everything would be better then. "Oh no, don't do that. I have to go. I just wanted to give you the doll," he said as he walked away and got into his car. Once again, I had messed things up and I didn't know how to fix it. "Please Daddy please", was all I could say as I watched him drive away for the last time. For many years I was left thinking that my own Dad didn't think I was pretty anymore, not realizing he was referring to the consequence of their divorce.

Chapter 8

Our television set stopped working. Mum called a repairman and that began a whole new phase in our lives. Edward Brown, owner of Brownwell's television repairs, came to fix it. He seemed to be a nice, trim, bald man, about our Mum's age. He had fixed the Maxwell's television, that was how Mum knew of him. While working on the Maxwell's television the problem was found to be in their antenna that was on the roof. Edward had to replace the antenna and had hired Pat to go up on the roof to assist him. This was how we could afford to get our TV repaired. Unfortunately, while helping, Pat had fallen from the roof onto the grass. He had insisted that he was unhurt in order to keep his new job. However, he would suffer back problems later in life, and he blamed them on that fall. Maybe we should have taken that fall as a warning from the universe!

Pat continued working with Edward doing antenna jobs and sometimes painting houses. It was good money for Pat, paying better than his newspaper jobs, and Mum seemed to enjoy Edward's company as he would stay to have a cup of tea with her after work. Today, Pat had worked with Edward and, since tomorrow was the first day of school, we were going to have a special dinner. Mum asked Edward to join us. It felt very strange to have a man at our dinner table, and I know most of us were uncomfortable, but we wanted to make it special for our Mum so we were on our best behavior.

Corinne and I were excused from the table first so that we could have our bath together in the claw- footed bathtub. It was the only bath in our only bathroom. Everyone had to be organized to each have our time needed in this room. After brushing our teeth and getting into our flannelette nightgowns, we went to say goodnight to everyone. Corinne and I each got our hug and kiss from Mum, Pat, Amanda (who had announced at dinner tonight that she no longer wished to be called Amanda but instead wanted to be called Lynn, her second name) and Scott. That left Edward who smiling said, "Don't I get a hug and kiss goodnight too?" Something in me wanted to scream, "NO!" but that would hurt his feelings and Mum would be ashamed of me. There was something about him that made me uncomfortable. I don't believe that I was shallow enough to feel uncomfortable to be hugged by him just because he was bald and I didn't know any other bald people, but there really was no reason that I could think of to explain my discomfort. I looked at Corinne and she looked at me. Somehow, we felt safer together and, like good little girls, we gave him a hug and a kiss.

"Wake up, Hanna. It's time to get ready for school," whispered my Mum into my ear. I was sleepy but the word "school" woke me up instantly! I felt that I had been waiting forever to go to school with my brothers and sisters and the day was finally here! I jumped out of bed so quickly that I was a little dizzy and it made my Mum giggle, "Come downstairs and have breakfast first, sleepyhead."

My clothes were waiting neatly on the end of my bed for me to put on. There was the pretty pink skirt with the white kittens that Cathy had given me for my birthday and a white blouse that used to be Corinne's. I reached for them to start dressing when Corinne said, "You don't get dressed until you've had breakfast first, in case you spill." I would have thought of that, except I was tired and excited.

I raced to the kitchen to find that "Lynn" was just leaving to catch her bus to the high school she went to. Pat was already gone on his paper route and would catch the bus from where he finished to the same school as Lynn. Scott was finished his breakfast and was feeding Cocoa. He wanted to leave a little earlier to play road hockey with his friends before class.

Waiting for me on the table was a steaming bowl of cream of wheat with brown sugar and canned milk, and a glass of powdered milk to drink. I was so full of excitement that I didn't feel like I could eat a bite but Mum wanted me to at least try. Corinne arrived to eat her bowl of cereal. "You don't look so good, Tink. Are you scared?" she asked me. "I was my first day and then I just hated it from that day on. Did you know that I even skipped out one day in Kindergarten? I hid in the ditch behind the house. I would have gotten away with it but I got too hungry and thought it would be after school time so I came out, but it was really only recess time!"

This made me laugh and helped me to feel a little better already. I was able to finish my breakfast and ran to brush my teeth in the bathroom, then headed upstairs to get dressed. I was anxious to get going but, with it being my first day, Mum was going to walk with us through the forest, so we had to wait a minute for her.

Finally, it was time to go. It was a long ½ mile walk, through the forest, up hills and down. It was very beautiful amongst the trees but it called to me to get dirty. I knew that I could sit and slide down some of those hills and it would be faster and easier but my clothes would get dirty. "Come on, slowpoke. You don't want to be late on your first day," warned my Mum. I was actually getting a little tired and was glad to see the end of the forest and the sidewalk in front of the school.

"Well Corinne, I guess you go to the gymnasium and I'll take Hanna to the kindergarten room. Scott will walk home with you after school, so you wait for him," said Mum giving Corinne a kiss on the cheek. I suddenly realized that we were not all going to be in the same room at school! My tummy felt a little tight in that second. Mum walked me to my room which had its own outside door. She held my hand as we walked down the stairs and turned into the open doorway of MY classroom! It was actually very nice with many tables with chairs around them, a playhouse at the back with an ironing board, a buggy, a crib and dishes all small enough for us kids.

"Good morning. I am Mrs. Sooters," said a pretty lady with black hair. She was wearing a green skirt with a white blouse. "Good morning. I am Mrs. Rutherford and this is my daughter, Hanna." "You can pick Hanna up here at the doorway at 10:30 today and for this week. Next week the class will extend to the usual time of 9-12 noon. I will send a list of supplies home today that will be needed for next week. You'll see your Mum later, Hanna. Now I'll show you the hook to hang your coat on in the cloakroom." We turned a corner in the room and there was a long row of hooks on each side of a narrow room. Above the hooks was writing and above that was a wooden box. We walked down the row until I saw my name "Hanna Rutherford" above one of the hooks. I knew what my name looked like from playing school with Corinne. "Is that my hook?" I asked. "That's good you recognized your name. Yes, that is where you will hang your coat. You will put your lunch kit, mittens and things in the box above the hook. Now you can go find yourself a place to sit at one of the tables until all of the children have arrived," and with this said, she left me.

I went from the cloakroom into the classroom, which was filling up with children. I chose a seat at the table like the teacher had asked. There was a girl sitting next to me, and a boy across the table from me. I remembered that when Corinne and I played school, you were not allowed to talk so I didn't talk to them. I wasn't shy. I just didn't want to get into trouble. Once everyone learned where his or her coat hooks were, the teacher brought us each a little bottle of milk. It was real milk like the men brought us at Christmas, not powdered milk like we drank at home, and two oatmeal cookies. She then explained that each day we would have a snack break but we were to bring our own snack and .25 to buy the milk. We were also to bring a pair of slippers to leave in our box above our coat hook and an apron for when we did painting. She gave us a piece of paper with this all written on in case we forgot. Then our school day was over! I was shocked it seemed that we had just gotten there. I got my coat from my hook and carried my paper to the door where Mrs. Sooters was checking each of us had our coats on. We said "Good-bye."

I followed the boy in front of me, up the stairs outside and I saw my Mum waiting.

"Well, don't you look like a real school girl now? Did you have fun? What's that paper you're carrying?" questioned my Mum. She started walking away from the school as if to go home but I stopped her by asking, "Where's Corinne? We have to wait for her." "No," she said. "Corinne has to stay in school longer than you. She will walk home with Scott later."

The walk home seemed much faster than the walk to school that morning. I had so much to tell Mum about all the children in my class and the teacher. Before I knew it, we were home. I changed out of my school clothes back into my play clothes. Mum fixed me a peanut butter and jam sandwich with a glass of powdered milk. It didn't taste as good after the real milk at school. I wanted to go outside to play with Darren but Mum thought that I should rest watching TV first and then I could go out. I just saw the opening of the show and I was asleep!

When I awoke, Art Linkletter was on. I usually liked to watch the kids but today I just wanted to go tell Darren all about my class. When I got to his house, his Mum told me that he was in the afternoon kindergarten and would be leaving in 10 minutes. I would have to go tell someone else about my day. Mr. Martin was the first person I saw.

"Hello, Mr. Martin. I just got home from school!" I boasted.

"You're full of prunes," he said, "If you were in school you wouldn't be done yet. School gets out at 3 o'clock."

"Well, I'm in kindergarten and it gets out earlier." I countered.

"You're full of prunes. You're too big for kindergarten." He responded

Mr. Martin always made me giggle, "No, I'm just tall for my age."

"Full of prunes is what you are! Mrs. Martin will want to know what you've been up to." He said.

He was right, as soon as Mrs. Martin saw me she asked, "Where have you been, I missed you this morning?" Over two peanut butter cookies I told all about my new school, feeling as snug as a bug!

Next, I went to tell Cathy. She was sitting in her metal toy car that had pedals inside but she wasn't big enough to reach them to make the car go. I got quite out of breath pushing her around while telling her all about my school. Her Mum came out just at that time to say, "Thanks for pushing Cathy around and keeping her so happy but it's her nap time now, so I'm afraid you'll have to go Hanna."

"That's okay. I was done anyway. Bye Cathy." I said as I waved good-bye.

Walking home I stopped at Mr. Evan's to tell him my news. I heard him coughing in the garage so I knew he was home. He saw me first and shouted, "Hey, Ladybug, where have you been?"

"It was my first day of school today!" I answered happily. I told him all about my classroom with the cloakroom and the hooks with our names above them.

"My goodness, you have to slow down a little, for us old guys to catch up!" he laughed.

Then I heard my Mum calling me in for dinner. She knew that I would hear her, being just next door, as Cocoa was at the Evan's doorstep. "Sorry, Mr. Evan, I have to go in."

Everyone was home now and I was so happy. We all had stories to tell about our first day of school in our various grades. Our dinner conversation was so full and special! I stayed a long time after everyone else was finished, and had already left the table, to tell Pat every detail of my day. He would always listen, encourage me and make me feel important. He was my father figure. I showed him the letter the teacher had given me for our supplies list. "Don't worry about this. Mum and I will talk about it," he said. I was not worried. I didn't even know what was on the paper. I had just given it to my Mum and that was what the teacher had told me to do. I said, "Goodnight" and went to brush my teeth and get my nightie on. Mum and Pat pondered over my list of requirements for a while. The apron was not a problem. Mum would give me one of hers. The slippers to leave at school were the problem. I would need to have new ones and we needed them by next Monday.

"Oh, I know," sighed Mum. "I have that knitting pattern for some quick and easy slippers. I am sure I would have enough spare wool to make ones big enough for Hanna's feet."

Chapter 9

That first year of school, Mum walked me home every day, as my siblings were still in class until much later. I loved school and the days passed quickly. I have great memories of painting on an easel, wearing my Mum's apron, playing house, listening to stories, playing with blocks, and snack time. The things I didn't like that year were nap times, every day for half an hour, and having our hearing tested. For the hearing test, the nurse came and got us four at a time. We went to another part of the school where we individually went into a room to put earphones on and tell the operator when we heard the beep. I sat very nervously waiting for my turn, feeling sicker and more upset with each child that went in. When it was my turn, I ran for my life, heading straight for Corinne's classroom, bursting in the door and right onto her lap crying! They excused Corinne from her class to come with me to do the test, which was very easy and not painful. To this day, I don't know what had been in my head about that test but I truly felt that I would die if I didn't hear the beep! Instead I just had to live with Corinne being embarrassed by me again.

After school was filled with my friends, neighbors, and family. Things were calmer with our Dad gone, but there was little to no money. Our Dad seldom sent his support payments and, what little money the paper route and antennae work Pat and Scott got, was stretched to the limits. My nights were less bothered with dreams of the crushing pink ball but now a new nightmare began. It revolved around a mechanical, black, Scotty dog that could bite through anything! It didn't matter where I was or whom I was with in the dream, the dog would appear. At Cathy Smith's house, on the school bus with Pat, I would always be running away from it and its steel jaws would bite through the walls trying to get to me. I awoke exhausted and terrified, afraid to sleep the next night!

Summer time was soon upon us and I noticed that Edward was like a household fixture now. Always picking up or dropping off one of the boys from antennae work, sometimes helping out with a chore we couldn't do around the house, like cleaning the eaves, and always staying for tea with Mum. He was always nice but there was something about him that my tummy didn't like. Maybe it was his baldhead, or the way that his cologne smelled, or the grimacing laugh he had, I don't know, it was just one of those feelings I tried to deny but couldn't.

In what seemed to be the blink of an eye, the summer was done and I was starting the first day of grade one! My teacher was a very nice lady, Miss Green. She told us which desk to sit in by what our last names were. I think she said it was "alfabitical". I was the first person in the second row from her desk. The desk was much different from the table and small chairs we had in kindergarten. Sitting in my desk my feet were about 4 inches from the floor! The room was alive with letters of the alphabet, a capital of the letter and a small letter, each with a picture of an animal that's name started with that letter. At recess and lunch time I was disappointed by the playground rules. The girls had to play on one side of the school and the boys on the other! Darren and I couldn't play together? I couldn't play with my best friend? That made no sense to me, but it was a school law.

By the second week, my classroom was beginning to feel quite comfortable, until a new girl came. We were all in our desks that morning when the janitor brought in an extra desk. "You can put it right here," Miss Green said signaling with her hands right in front of me. I liked being the first person in my row but now I'd be second. A few minutes later this girl showed up. "Class we have a new girl joining us. Her name is Carolyn Miles, would you say hello to welcome her, please." Everyone said in unison, "Hello Carolyn." I know that I felt slighted by her because she got my place but I later found out she was my cousin to me (on my Dad's side of the family) and so had to put that aside.

Christmas was in the air again. We were doing Christmas puzzles in Arithmetic and Reading. I really liked these. For Arithmetic, there would be a picture of a Christmas tree with an addition question at the end of a branch. If the answer was 3 you would color that Christmas ball red, if the answer was 4, color it blue, etc. In Reading, the puzzle would be a stocking with a stripe to be colored red if the kitten's name was Puff, blue if the kitten's name was Spot.

We were all excited at home because that weekend we were having Aunt Irene, Uncle Amos, Aunt Bernice, and Uncle Sigmond over for a Christmas dinner. They were two of the six aunts and uncles from my father's family that we still saw. We all got dressed in our best clothes. Pat and Scott had cleaned out what was Lynn's bedroom, at that time, to make room to set our kitchen table. We added some plywood across 2 saw horses to make the table larger so we could all eat in there together. Corinne and I, under Lynn's supervision had set the tables with tablecloths, napkins, knives and forks, plates, glasses and Christmas crackers. I had never even seen a Christmas cracker before. Mum and Lynn had made a great dinner of turkey, stuffing, mashed potatoes, vegetables, gravy and Christmas pudding for dessert. A most festive occasion, which I almost destroyed when, I piped up and asked, "What does fuck mean?"

The room was suddenly silent! Pat's hand slid down from the table, encompassing mine, as he said in a firm, steady voice, "Come with me."

We walked hand in hand into the next bedroom where he turned and closed the door behind us. "So where did you hear that word?" he asked. "I didn't. I read it on a store wall," I answered.

"Don't read things from store walls!" was all he said. We walked back and finished a great dinner. He never answered my question, but I never read store walls again.

We celebrated a quiet Christmas. Not a lot of commercialism, but more importantly time together.

Chapter 10

Lynn, Scott, Corinne and I returned to school after the New Year began. Pat didn't have to go to school anymore because he had graduated. He had also turned 19 on his December birthday. He would often come to walk Corinne and I home. This I loved because I could tell him all about my day while we walked. Today, we had left a saucer filled with a little water on the counter. The teacher said that it was our science project, to see what would happen to the water overnight. "We have to wait until tomorrow to find out" I said completely baffled.

At dinner that evening I heard mention of Pat going away to some school. He looked at me so earnestly and said, "Tink, how do you feel about that?" I felt this could not be happening, it wasn't real. Were they just trying to test me to see if I would behave if I thought this was true? "Okay," slipped from my lips. I remember that he tried to explain how he was going to the Academy to become a policeman but it was too much for me to take in. I could not foresee my life without Pat! It just couldn't happen.

The next morning, I awoke feeling anxious to get to school. I couldn't wait to see what happened to the water! I was dressed and at the breakfast table in record time. Pat was sitting there all dressed up in a suit he had borrowed from Mr. McGregor. "Are you going to walk me to school to see what happened to the water," I asked. "No, Tink. I have to leave for the airport in an hour." Why was he still trying to test me? I knew he would never go!

I finished my breakfast with what felt like the weight of an iron between my eyebrows. I excused myself to go brush my teeth and get my shoes on for school. When I came back into the living room, Pat was standing next to a huge suitcase with his arms outstretched to me, "Well

Tink, this is it. Can I have a hug good-bye?" I knew he could not be going. That would be like the morning not coming after the night. It could not be, but I gave him a little kiss and hug even though my whole body inside felt like that heavy iron. I left with Corinne for the long walk to school. My thoughts focused on the mysterious dish of water and the heavy iron started to disappear.

Edward and Mum drove Pat to the airport so he could fly out that day. Pat had never been in an airplane before. That morning the airport was completely fogged in, much the same as Pat's head felt, filled with mixed emotions of excitement and dread. The fog began clearing just in time for his flight, a good sign.

As long as he could remember, he had always wanted to be a policeman. To make things right and fair like his favorite character in the western television show. When application forms to join the Police came to his school to entice grade twelve graduates, he jumped at the chance. He just made the height requirement of 5'11" and he passed all the other stipulations. Today they were flying him to the training academy for 18 months. He had longed to get away, to be free of his family obligations that should never have belonged to him. Edward had come into his Mother's life at just the right time. They were planning to marry this August, and he felt this was the answer for his family to be well taken care of while he got on with his own life. So why was he feeling so apprehensive?

"Flight 247 now boarding at gate 3," came over the announcements.

His bag already checked Pat said, "That's me. I've got to go." Giving his Mum a gentle hug he said, "Mum, you take care of yourself and all of those kids. It's time for you to start enjoying your life." And he kissed her cheek good-bye.

"Pat, I love you, son. Take care of yourself and don't worry about us!" She gave him the mightiest hug she could muster, as she felt her first born leave her home.

The flight was very picturesque. The beautiful blue water dotted with many islands with their towering green trees. Within minutes he saw the towering buildings and bridges of a big city. "Fasten your seat belts and prepare for landing," announced the stewardess. His connecting flight for the academy left in just 40 minutes so he needed to collect his suitcase and get to the next gate. Once he was aboard and air bound his thoughts were on his future. What would the experience be like? He was very excited about training with the horses. He thought that he had inherited his maternal grandfather's love of the noble beasts. Paul Applegate had always been the Clydesdales groomsman at a manor in England.

Again, Pat's thoughts returned, unwillingly, to his family. He imagined each of their faces gathered around in their sparsely furnished old house and he felt immense guilt. He could try to convince himself a million times, that he was leaving them at the right time, to give Edward his place to act as father, but it just didn't feel okay!

He thought back over his life and what had brought him to this point. He had never been away from his family home since he was 3 years old and our Mother, three- month-old Amanda and he had immigrated to Canada from England at the end of the war. Our father had been a Canadian army private drafted to England, where he had met our Mother. They were married and she became known as a "war bride".

After the war, the families of enlisted men were sent home first to ensure their safety before the men were transported. This was a terrible time for our Mother, having to say good-bye to her parents and sister possibly forever! She then would be 3 weeks aboard a rolling ship with a tiny baby and an active toddler. She arrived in a strange land, to board a train for 3 days to continue travelling further away from all that was familiar! After the train journey, she was told, along with other wives, to collect their bags for transport by bus to the ferry terminal. The trip still had not ended? Thank goodness little Patrick was so helpful pushing Amanda's stroller while Mum carried their bags. Out of shear exhaustion, the three of them slept quite soundly on the overnight ferry crossing.

Waking refreshed thankfully, our Mother starting tidying her small children and herself to meet their new family. When the ship touched shore, they saw they were in a quaint little bay, banked by several beautiful buildings. Quite irrelevant now as all that mattered was to find the Rutherford family. Surely all this travel would be worth it when her family would all be together with Chad. First, they were to meet the family.

Chad senior with his second wife, Alice, met them at the ferry terminal. Dagney could see that Chad had characteristics from each of his parents. His narrow face and slight build from his Mother and his dark hair and eye color from his father. Neither parent had the happy-go-lucky stance of their son though. They both appeared very uninterested and cold. Not the welcoming Mum had hoped for! The drive to their home was very quiet and uncomfortable.

Finally, they arrived and could disembark and get some space from each other.

"The rest of the family is here to meet you, of course," informed Alice. As if on cue, the front door opened and the people poured out. "Let's get indoors and then I'll do the introductions," Alice announced proudly.

Amanda, who had been a model baby to travel with, was just starting to fuss for her feeding. "Do you think the introductions could wait until after Amanda and I have a quiet room to ourselves so I can nurse her?" asked Dagney. "Oh, you can't feed her by bottle? Everyone has been waiting so patiently to meet you." Alice said in exasperation. "I'm sorry the baby can't wait, she just won't settle if I don't feed her first," answered our Mother as she, with baby in arms and little Patrick in tow, hurried passed the throng of people blocking the doorway and into an empty bedroom, shutting the door behind them.

"Well, we've been put in our place! I guess this is how it will be with this stranger in our midst!" angrily responded Alice, the matriarch of the family. From this moment on there was tension between these two women. Amanda was fed, diapered and settled to sleep on the clean bed with pillows all around to stop her from rolling off. Patrick had eaten an apple and had his face washed. Now they were ready to meet their new family.

Dagney opened the bedroom door, took little Patrick's hand, and nervously approached the closed glass door to the parlor. Unsure whether to knock, as an outsider, or just to enter as a member of the family she faltered for a moment and was judged by some. A man on the inside jumped to his feet, opening the door and extended his hand to our Mother saying, "Let me introduce myself and welcome you to Canada. I am Paul, Chad's youngest brother, and if I may, I will introduce the rest of this brood. I will start with Chad's eldest brother, Rod and his wife Elna, I think we'll introduce all of the children next time. Then there is his sister Jenny and her husband Roy, sister Bernice and her husband Sigmond, sister Irene and husband Amos. Chad is the next born followed by Pauline who lives out of Province with her husband, Larry, and then there's my wife, Lynn and I.

"Wow! We used to just have Grand mama, Grandpapa, and Aunt Joan in our family back home. Now we have all kinds of family!" marveled little Patrick in his English accent. A gentle laugh filled the room and someone said, "I love that British accent." Then in that accent Patrick stammered, "I'm not British, I'm Canadian!" and the gentle laugh became a roar!

When Chad returned home to his family from the war, he was never quite himself again. To some it was because of his wife and children. To others it was because of his overbearing Mother, or the war, or alcohol, or a multitude of reasons. Pat and Mum never felt accepted by the grandmother, who was rumored to have never believed that Pat and Amanda were Chad's children. Did she really think that Dagney had entrapped him into marriage? That was all so long ago, Pat, don't think of these things now.

Pat spent the rest of his flying time, remembering many happy hours spent camping and fishing with these aunts and uncles. He had learned many things from car repairs, tying fishing flies, making Indian beadwork, setting up camps to cleaning fish. These were always his favorite trips. He had enjoyed the time spent with these good people and always wondered how they didn't see the mostly verbal, but often physical, abusiveness of his father.

He thought now, of the last camping trip he had been on with his Dad. Just his immediate family went to Cowichan River near Duncan, an hour drive north of Victoria. The first day began with setting up camp. It always took a few hours to unpack the trailer, decide where to position the tents and then put them up. The coolers, filled with huge blocks of ice, and all the food we would need, were set in the shadiest spots.

When this was done, our father said, 'I'm just going to run to the store for some smokes," and that was the last we saw of him for two weeks. We enjoyed our days hiking, fishing at the river, playing ball, or board games and berry picking, but our Mother never relaxed for a moment. When we ran out of food and our Dad was still not back, she didn't know how we were to get home. The only person she knew that owned a car was the television repairman that Pat had worked for, and she felt that she didn't know him well enough to ask such a big favor. Her children's hungry tummies gave her courage to phone and ask. We all walked the half mile to the phone booth while Mum called and she told us, "He will be here in an hour so we must hurry and pack up!" We had everything packed and in boxes beside the road by the time Edward arrived. Our father had taken the trailer with the car when he left so all of our supplies had to be squashed into the back of Edward's station wagon, four kids in the back seat and Mum and Hanna in the front seat.

Chapter 11

As soon as I reached my classroom I saw the crowd of people around the saucer which was empty! Someone must have spilled it and our experiment was ruined. Then Miss Green entered the room and asked us to please take our seats. No one told her about the dish being empty for fear that she would be angry.

"I see you were all looking at the saucer and that you were very interested in our experiment. What did you see had happened?" she asked.

"Somebody wrecked it by dumping the water out," said a big boy in our class.

"Is that the conclusion you came to? What about the rest of the class? What do you think happened?" inquired Miss Green. "Hanna?"

I was afraid and didn't want her to start blaming people for spilling it so I suggested, "Maybe a cat came in and drank it?"

With a slight chuckle she replied, "I guess that could have happened but, being on the second floor with the windows and doors closed, I doubt it. No, I will tell you what happened. Something drank the water but it wasn't a living thing, it was the air! It is called evaporation." To a gasp of astonishment by all, she continued. "You see science has many surprises in store for you. It is my favorite subject and I think it might be yours as well."

The rest of the day was filled with Reading, Arithmetic and Printing but I just couldn't wait to get home to tell Pat what happened to the water!

As soon as I saw Corinne playing Hop Scotch with her friends, I told her, "The air drank the water in our experiment. We have to hurry home so I can tell Pat." "Pat's not there! Remember he told you he was going into the Police Academy today?" she told me, looking quite annoyed that I would have forgotten. We started off for home right away and I felt my body full of iron again. I didn't say a word all the way, but I could hear Corinne and her friend talking as if they were far away in the background.

When I spotted our house, I ran in through the kitchen door calling, "Pat! Pat!"

Mum appeared, "Oh Hanna, Pat's not here. Remember he told you he was leaving today for the academy?" she spoke so softly, yet the words were so heavy they pushed me to the ground. I lay there on my knees on the kitchen floor as if praying to something to let me live and breathe, sobbing. Mum came to try to lift me up but I slid through her arms so as not to hear what she was telling me. He could not be gone! I ran to his room where his bed was made as if he were home. I looked out the window to see if he was working in the back yard on his car. I could not see him anywhere but I would wait on his bed until he returned. His pillow smelled of him and I knew that he would be home. He had to be, he was my stability.

I awoke to Mum saying, "Hanna, will you come and have something to eat for supper?" I had the hiccups from crying and the last thing I felt like was eating. "Is Pat home yet?" I begged. "He will not be home for many months, Hanna. He tried to tell you before he went. He is a grown man now and he has to go find his own way in life. I'm sure he will miss you too, but he will write and come home when he can." Even today to write these words brings tears to my eyes. I still miss him as my mentor, my big brother, father figure, protector, and friend.

For the next two days, we did not see our dog Cocoa, and heavy snows were falling. He would not come when we called him. On the third day, Edward and Scott went looking in the forest for him. They found him just lying on a rock ledge, mostly covered in snow. He too, was pining for Pat, and would have stayed there until he died. Edward and Scott took turns carrying his dead weight back home. They put him in his favorite spot, behind the old oil stove, to thaw. The stove was about 3 feet wide by 5 feet high. It had white ceramic panels, oven door, and warming oven above. There was a shelf for putting spices on and a heavy cast iron cooking surface with rings to lift in and out. The rings each had a metal hook that was wrapped in chrome to keep the handle cool. You could lift the rings out to check the intensity of the fire; it made a warm barricade to hide behind.

For days, we tried to feed Cocoa by hand. Finally, we felt hopeful with the first lick of his tongue. He would eat a small mouthful now, then a little more the next time, in a few days he would eat the usual bowl full. In a few weeks, Cocoa was recovered and back to his old self, as if nothing had happened. Life continued on its path, but never did our home feel quite full or complete again.

Chapter 12

"Please put your seat in the upright position we are about to land," whispered the stewardess to Pat. Suddenly he was filled with apprehension and excitement. Could this really be happening? With a screech, the wheels of the jet touched ground and Pat had arrived. He felt so foreign, unsure and yet thrilled at the prospects ahead of him. He quickly rose to his feet and opened the overhead compartment to gather his belongings. He took down his overnight bag, checking inside the zippered compartment for his family photo. "You see guys. I didn't really leave you behind. I will always have you with me." He thought to himself.

The recruiting officer had told him, that once he had retrieved his luggage he was to wait outside the regional flights arrivals door. This he did as quickly as possible.

"Cadet Rutherford?" snapped a baritone voice. Turning, Pat saw a tall man, in his mid-thirties in police uniform.

"Follow me, please." He continued. Pat quickly picked up his suitcase and shoulder bag and raced to catch up to the man. Within moments, they had cleared at least 100 yards and were in front of a row of young men, all standing next to their suitcases, Pat fell in line.

"I am Sergeant Wells from the Training Academy. I will have you follow me to the bus that will transport you to the barracks. You will put all luggage in the luggage compartment underneath the bus and board the bus, filling it from back to front. There is to be no talking, lest you should miss any further instructions." commanded the Sergeant. "Move."

Mere seconds passed and the bus was underway. Pat wondered if they left anyone behind and heaven help the man if they did. The ride to the academy was long and tedious with no conversation, only the occasional points of interest told to them by Sergeant Wells. "Now, we are entering the grounds to the academy and you will need to listen so you will be able to find your way around. That large building on the left is the mess hall where you will eat. You will want to remember where that one is! The smaller building across from it is the officer's mess where you are not to be! To our right is the motor pool where all of our vehicles are serviced. You will learn how to perform regular maintenance on them. This will be vital in many circumstances, for your own squad car or in assisting stranded members of the public. The building we are now passing is the shooting range where you will receive instruction on how to load, fire and maintain your weapon. The white building on the left is the infirmary, where you report any illnesses or injuries. Next to this is the gymnasium, where you will get most of your injuries. Then there is the clothing warehouse, should you need replacements by turning in the old item. This is the stable, where we exercise, groom and feed our horses. You will be introduced to your horse next week. This will be your horse for the next 18 months. We give you a week to adjust before we add the responsibility of grooming and feeding a horse on top of your other expectations.

This square, brick building that we are pulling up in front of is 'A' block, home of 'A' troop who is Ralph Andrews, Rick Aldersmith, Brian Aggers, Gary Billings, Howard Brisboise, Michael Crane, Mark Dean, Patrick Edwards, Clifford Easter and Paul Frost. All of those men named please, exit the bus, collect your luggage and proceed into 'A' block. This was done without much ado and the bus proceeded to the next square brick building which Sergeant Wells announced as 'B' block" and called, "Peter Glassel, Victor Granger, Derrick Hall, Bruce Halbourgh, Donald Horn, Robert Hannibal, Daniel Isaac and Bent Jorgensen. Once again, the exit was done with precision and the bus moved on. As expected, at the next brick building, Sergeant Wells piped up, "'C' block, Daryl Kane, Martin Kyle, Benjamin Larsen, Rudolph Leighton, Neil Lunn, Trevor Malkin, William Martin, Erick Milton, Paul Noland and Pat Rutherford. Disembark, retrieve your luggage and proceed into 'C' block." Pat felt alien to his surroundings and his mind was filled with thoughts of home and family. He proceeded as instructed into block 'C'. Inside, he joined the line of men with luggage beside them.

Another uniformed man stood before them and he said, "I am Corporal Benson, your unit or squad leader. I will direct you to your room and bunk assignments. Follow me, bringing your luggage with you." They marched together, stopping outside an open doorway. "Daryl Kane, Martin Kyle, Benjamin Larsen, Rudolph Leighton and Neil Lunn this is your room. You will find your name attached to everything that belongs to you. You may put all of your belongings away into your dresser and cupboards. I suggest that you do this quickly as the dinner bell will be sounding soon. When you hear it, please assemble in the front foyer for further orders." The five men listed fell out of line and raced into their room. The remaining five followed Corporal Benson to the next open doorway. "This, of course, is your room men. The same applies to you. Only what has your name on it is yours and you have even less time to unpack before the dinner bell rings."

Inside was a very orderly room containing five beds. Each bed was accompanied with a mirrored closet and a small night table with lamp and alarm clock. There was a large wooden chest at the foot of each bed. The beds were meticulously made with a brown wool blanket and a yellow pillowcase. Each man hurried to their bed area and began to unpack. Pat unpacked his suitcase into the closet and he placed his folded items into the wooden chest. His family photo, he placed carefully onto the bedside table. Again, he felt a sick empty feeling. The dinner bell sounded and he quickly stuffed his empty suitcase into the closet. His shoulder bag still held his toiletry items, so he left it on the bed until later when he would know where to unpack them and he ran to the foyer.

Charging into the foyer he heard Corporal Benson say, "So glad you could join us, Cadet Rutherford. During your first 6 months at the academy, you will be expected to run everywhere you go. Now, we will run to the mess hall. As you were instructed to pay attention to directions as you entered the grounds, we will expect that you will know how to get to the mess hall. Lead off." The men, leading the group leaving C block, chose to head left from the front of the building. Pat felt that they should have gone right but, as the group started to run, Pat thought maybe he was mistaken. He chose to follow. After jogging for 40 minutes, they arrived at the mess hall exhausted. Pat felt almost sick to his stomach from gulping air and now had to eat. He noticed that the men who had gone right, were almost finished their dinners and looking rested! He would be sure to trust his own instincts more in the future.

As he ate, he wondered what his family would have had for dinner. He couldn't help but feel hurt little Hanna hadn't seemed very sad to see him go. He knew that it was for the best though. How was Scott dealing with being the man of the house now? Lynn was now a beautiful young woman and would have many boyfriends. Would she be careful? Corinne was so mischievous, he knew that she would always have fun, but would she stay out of trouble? Maybe I should never have left them, he felt.

"Attention!" shouted Sergeant Wells. "Dinner break is over. You will put your garbage into the allocated bins, put your dirty dishes into the appropriate racks and wipe both your table area and tray with a clean dishrag. Then return your tray to the pile. Once done, return to your barracks for timetables and clothing allotments."

Having finished tidying up after his dinner, Pat started running back to his barracks in the direction he thought would be best. In just 10 minutes he was there! In the foyer, was a long table with piles of folded clothing. On top of each pile was a piece of paper with a man's name and timetable on it.

"Pick up your pile of clothing, and the shoes and sneakers in front of it," snapped Corporal Benson. "You will be expected in T shirt, shorts and sneakers for calisthenics in the gymnasium one hour before breakfast."

There was quite an armload of items: 3 T-shirts, 2 pairs of shorts and sweatpants, a warm flannel jacket with hood, and two pairs of shoes. As he walked back to his room, Pat was reading his timetable. Breakfast was at 0700 and gym was one-hour prior, that would mean he would have to set his alarm for 0515?! Then the day was packed with activities, 0800-1000 law class, 1100-1200 water skills in the pool, 1200-1300 lunch break, 1300-1400 firearms, 1400-1600 horsemanship, 1600-1700 automotive, 1700-1900 dinner break, 1900-2100 gym. His time was completely allotted.

"Cadet Rutherford! Your sleep area is to look just as you found it and that means nothing left on the bed!" shouted Corporal Benson. "Being that it's just your first day, it will only cost you 10 push-ups."

Pat was so startled. He stood dumbfounded trying to think what he had left on his bed.

"Now, Rutherford!" snapped Benson.

Welcome to the academy thought Pat!

"Let me show you where to put your toiletry items men," added Corporal Benson. "Follow me." At the end of the room there was an entrance into a large bathroom. The bathroom had 3 sinks, 3 urinals, one cubicle with toilet, and 2 shower stalls. On one wall, there were shelves on which they were told to put their shaving kits. Pat did not own a 'kit' but would soon buy one. For now, he embarrassedly put his unwrapped shaver, toothbrush holder, toothpaste, brush and comb naked on the shelf. Those old feelings of humiliation and worthlessness were back. Surely the academy does not train their recruits by belittling them!?

"You men had better be thinking of getting to bed. Morning comes early around here!" warned Corporal Benson.

It was 2100 hours. Pat undressed, set his alarm for 0515 and climbed into his cold, stark bed. His mind was flooded with images of his hectic day, starting at his old home. He saw the faces of his family that he missed so much. Hopefully they were all snug in their beds and were not worrying about him. How was Scott managing the paper routes? Pat fretted that it would be too much for Scott, who was 6 years younger than him. Lynn would have to take the city bus across town alone to school, would she be okay? Corinne was a sweet little imp but needed a guiding hand. Hopefully she wouldn't get lost along her way. Tink, oh little Tinkerbell, who would she tell her daily school stories to? She was filled with so much excitement that Pat never wanted her to lose it! Mum would have Edward now to help her with any problems but what did they really know about him? Pat's face felt drained of blood and his stomach felt full of guilt. Had he made a mistake in coming here? Had he abandoned his family? He turned to check the clock…2230! He had to be up in just 5 and 3/4 hours! He would have a full day tomorrow and would need his rest. If only he could sleep!

Chapter 13

"BEEP, BEEP, BEEP!" He looked at the alarm. Could it be 5:15 already? His day began quickly, marched on even faster following his timetable, and ended in exhaustion but still, thoughts of home haunted him, and he could not sleep! His fatigue was noticed at the next morning's gym class.

"Keeping you up, are we, Rutherford?" taunted Sergeant Wells.

"I had a little trouble sleeping, Sir." responded Pat.

"Homesick or is the bed not soft enough for your liking? You better sleep tonight or you'll be in the infirmary tomorrow!" After gym class, Sergeant Wells pulled Pat aside, "Seriously Cadet, you need your rest. Being your commanding officer, I am responsible for you so we need to get to the bottom of the problem!"

"Well sir, I hope I haven't made a terrible mistake in coming here," stammered Pat. "You see I have always been responsible for my 4 siblings and my Mother. With her new fiancé in the picture I thought this would be my chance to leave."

"And you don't feel that way now?" asked Wells.

"I'm not sure. I just need to call home."

"You are allowed to make only one call to home, so make sure you get all the information you need to clear your mind. If you decide that your family needs you and you wish to return to them, I think that you need to realize your dilemma. The Police were needing men, so your flight here was paid, but you would have to reimburse us for that and pay for your flight home if you leave, a total of $620," warned Wells.

"I understand. I would still like to call." Pat went to the payphone in C block's foyer and asked the operator to place a collect call to his Mother's phone number. She accepted the call, fearing the worst! Pat was ashamed to admit why he had called, saying the academy just wasn't for him and having to beg for a loan to get him home. He knew his Mother would have to ask Edward for a loan until Pat could pay him back. She said they would have to talk it over and took the number to call back tomorrow. Pat related this to Sergeant Wells, who suggested Pat pick up and continue on with his timetable until the call came tomorrow. Pat gladly did this, slipping into his law class halfway through. He enjoyed his whole day and slept much better that night, believing he would be going home in a day or two.

"What? Pat called?" Lynn asked excitedly. "No, no. We were just talking about him," responded Edward. "I wish he would call. It's been 3 days now and I'd like to hear how he's doing." answered Lynn with a tear in her eye. Brother and sister had always been very close, both in good times and in bad. "It's awfully expensive to phone. I'm sure he will only phone when he has something really important to tell us." said Mum, always the voice of reason. "Dinner is already made, Lynn. We are having homemade chicken soup with bread. So, you might as well eat and then go get your homework done right away." "Good idea. I have a huge English project due in a few days and it will be a lot of work!" she excused herself to go to her room.

Mum and Edward continued to talk in muffled voices over their cups of tea. "Where are the rest of the kids? No point in upsetting them over this. We should keep it between us," said Edward. Mum agreed. "Scott is out delivering Pat's papers, Corinne and Hanna are up in their room playing something. Pat is requesting $620, which is a lot of money, but how could I deny him the right to come home? I love him so much and only want him to be happy." lamented our Mother. "We could send him the money if you think it's the right thing to do. My feeling is that when the going gets tough, the tough get going. I'm sure the academy training is very strict and demanding. Pat is probably a little overwhelmed by it, as well as missing his family. I think he will appreciate it, in the long run, if we help him to stick to it and not just bring him home where he didn't want to be in the first place." answered Edward.

"Oh, I just want to bring him home, but I guess that's just silly. I'm glad that I have you to help me make the decision. I had better make the call and get it over with." She dialed the number feeling like she was walking to the gallows. A very professional dignified voice answered, "Training Academy, Sergeant-Major Cooper here."

"Yes, I am calling to speak to my son who is a recruit," our Mother's voice quivered.

"Well ma'am they are all in classes at the moment. Could I take a message for you to pass on after class is done?" answered Sergeant-Major Cooper.

"Well, yes. His name is Pat Rutherford and the message is, there are no funds at this time. Sorry."

"I will pass that message during schedule break," the official voice responded, taking away any chance for her to speak with and make explanations to her son.

She slowly hung the phone back on its cradle. Her heart was too heavy to beat. She had always been so close to her son and now, suddenly, she felt the expanse of all the miles that he was away. Her breath came out only in a whisper as she said, "Well, I hope he takes it okay. I don't want him to feel uncared about now that I have a new man in my life."

"I'm sure that Pat wouldn't think such a thing. He'll know that it's for the best," spoke the new man in question. "Let's talk about something happier, like the wedding. I could pick up the invitations today and we could start sending them out. It is 5 months tomorrow until the date. Is it too early to send out the invitations?"

"We could start writing them and addressing them today. We won't mail them until they are all written and that could take a month or so itself. We could probably mail them 3 months in advance. That will give them time to get over the shock!" laughed Mum.

"What? The shock that Edward's finally getting married?" said Edward with downcast eyes.

"No. I meant the shock of you inheriting a whole family. I still can't believe you would marry me with 5 children! That takes a very special man."

Corinne and Hanna walked into the room. "Who's a special man?" asked Corinne.

"Edward. Not many men would marry a woman, then instantly become a father to 5 children!" explained Mum.

Corinne was deep in thought, "What will we call you after the wedding?" she said, looking at Edward.

This put him in an awkward position. If he said that he wanted to be called Dad, the children might be offended because they already had a dad. He didn't want them to call him Edward because then how could he discipline them if they thought of him as a friend and not as a father. "I want you to call me what you would like," was his reply.

To a little girl, who had recently seen her father walk out of her life and had said good-bye to her older brother who had been her acting father, this was not what she had hoped to hear. She needed so desperately for someone to want her and to want her to call them Dad!

When Pat had finished his dinner break and left the mess hall, he saw a large cork message board with a note that had his name pinned to it. He hurried over to unpin it, wondering how they would wire him the money. 'No funds at this time!' was written on the paper. In total shock, he thought, "do not let your knees buckle in front of the guys!" How could this happen? Do they not realize how important this is? I don't have another choice! What was he to do? Next on his schedule was gym class. He felt like a zombie. How could he go, but what else could he do? Somehow in his stupor he managed to get into his gym strip and report for duty.

Corporal Benson was just inside the door to the gym and motioned Pat aside, "I heard you got the reply and it wasn't what you expected. I hope you will do the honorable thing and continue on with the course."

Cadet Rutherford responded, "Certainly, sir!" but thought what else could he do. He had tried for so many years to earn his father's love and respect, and thought he'd failed. Now he would work his hardest to get it back from his family. He was sure that he had lost it by asking to come home. His path was in place now and there was no going back. He was such a gentle, caring man who kept getting mixed messages about life. He would knuckle down now and get himself through the training and make his family proud of him, so he could at least go home for visits.

Chapter 14

The next 5 months passed without incidence for us kids who were still at home. We all seemed to be knuckling down without enjoying the magic of childhood, as if somehow the wonder was gone. Mum was very busy with plans for the wedding. We all had to have a new outfit and shoes! As the day grew closer we also had to prepare for moving. After the wedding, we would be moving into a much newer house right on the water! One morning Mum had sorted out all of my clothing that I had outgrown and put them in a bag to go to Goodwill. Edward had put the bag on the back seat of his station wagon and gone back in the house for a second load. When he returned to the car Cocoa was sitting next to my clothes growling and snapping at Edward. Do dogs have a sixth sense? Should we have disregarded his warning as we did, just thinking that he was being over protective?

Later that day Edward had to drop a television set to one of his customers who lived way out in the country. He asked if we would like to go with him for the ride? Mum and I were the only ones to say that we would like to go. It was such a hot and muggy day! We had all of the windows down in the car but still I felt quite sick from the heat. Mum noticed my flushed cheeks and asked, "Are you feeling okay, Hanna?" "I'm just dizzy because it's too hot," I answered. "Do you want to take your shirt off? It would make you much cooler," she suggested. I quickly glanced at Edward. Had she forgotten he was there? "Oh, I'm sorry," she chuckled. "I forgot." "What? Oh, of course, you can take your shirt off," said Edward.

Feeling completely humiliated I looked down and tried to disappear. I knew my cheeks were flushed now, but not just from the heat. "Oh, don't worry about it then. Maybe we can stop at a store for a Popsicle or something cool," answered Mum. "What? Why can't she just take her shirt off?" Edward replied looking at Mum. "She's embarrassed because she's a little girl!"

"Well, that's silly, I'm almost her Dad. I will be after next weekend," retorted Edward sounding a little annoyed. "We know that, but little girls have their pride and modesty," Mum explained.

"This is plain stupid! It's not as if she has anything to show even!" snapped Edward. I had done it again. Caused trouble! Now it was between Mum and Edward but I just couldn't take my shirt off. I was too mortified.

Finally, we were at the customer's house. Edward stopped the car and got out, taking the television with him into the house. Mum and I just sat in silence, each of us thinking about what had just happened. Me blaming myself and Mum feeling sad for Edward who, she felt, just wanted to be treated as a Dad. We never spoke of the instance in the car and I never complained about being too hot again.

The next day a large 3 ft. square box arrived from Pat! Inside was a tastefully wrapped wedding gift for Mum and Edward and a short letter telling how busy he was with his training, how he wished that he could be with us all for the special day and how he was looking forward to our letters. It was so nice to hear from him. It made him feel close again if only for a moment. Mum and Edward opened their gift of pots n pans.

We had to go for haircuts before the wedding and we didn't go to the barber's like we usually did! This time Lynn, Corinne and I got to go with Mum to her hairdresser! My hair was still cut very short but not like a boy's cut this time.

The next day was the wedding. We all had to bathe and get dressed up in our new clothes. Mum had a beautiful tan colored, brocade, knee length dress with short sleeves and a matching hat. Lynn had a beautiful, pink, cotton dress, straight bodice with a flared skirt, cap sleeves and pretty white shoes. Corinne had a teal colored, cotton, tunic style, sleeveless dress. It had a little jacket in matching material with puffy, capped sleeves. She also had white, patent leather shoes with matching clutch purse. She wore a small, pill- box style, white hat matching Lynn's. I wore a little yellow taffeta dress with a mesh overlay showing my shoulders and upper arms. My shoes matched Corinne's and I wore a wide hair-band of tiny, white, silk flowers in my hair. I carried a little, white purse that had a clear plastic round base covered in white netting. I had never felt so elegant before.

Every time I stepped out the front door all of our neighbors cheered! I went outside quite a few times to savor this feeling. I had never felt pretty but I wished it was true. Corinne was embarrassed by my parading in and out, but I didn't care.

We rode in Edward's brother Frank's car, who was a stranger to me, to the church. I heard Lynn say, "See that building across the street? That is one of our Dad's favorite drinking places. Wouldn't it be something if he saw us? My heart started racing. When she said "one of our Dad's" what did she mean by one of our Dad's favorite drinking places? Did she mean our new Dad or our old Dad? If she meant our old Dad, I hoped that he would see us. Maybe he would think I was pretty today, enough to be his pretty little girl again? I felt very confused by what Lynn had said. I couldn't ask anyone about it now as we were moving into the church and so many people were talking about me.

After the service, we were loaded back into the cars and taken to another building for the reception. It was a beautiful, big building overlooking the water. The night went so fast, between exploring the building, checking out all of the little pastry goodies, and a man showing me some fireworks out over the water. I was watching these when Lynn came running out to me shouting, "Tink, we've been looking everywhere for you! Mum wanted to say good-bye to you before she has to leave with Edward for their honeymoon. Hurry, I hope they haven't gone already!" We raced through the building, out the back door, to the covered driveway where there were just 5 or 6 people saying, "Oh, you just missed them. They waited as long as they could but they had to go."

It wasn't long until we were again loaded into "Uncle Frank's" car and driven home. Inside the doorway, Mrs. Williams greeted us. I remembered meeting her last week. Mum had introduced her to us as the lady who would be looking after us while Mum and Edward were on their honeymoon. It was really happening! They were already gone and I didn't even say good-bye! That sick lead feeling was back in my stomach again.

For the next three days, I lay on the couch with a cold cloth on my head thinking I was dying. I could not eat for the sickness in my tummy. My life felt so empty with Pat and now Mum gone! Mrs. William's and my siblings were very good to me while our Mum was on her honeymoon with Edward.

The day they returned, they were driving an empty moving truck ready to take all of our belongings to our new home. I felt much better with Mum back but it was strange with Edward there all the time now. It didn't take more than a few hours to load the coach, chair, TV, our four children's beds, and the few boxes of dishes from the kitchen that we had. Mum and Edward had spent most of their honeymoon unpacking their wedding gifts and putting them where they belonged in our new home.

Edward and Scott drove the moving truck to our new home. After unloading all of our furnishing, they returned the truck to the moving and storage lot and went to pick up Mum at our old house. Stepping inside the kitchen doorway Edward met Mum with a kiss. "Did you manage to unload everything?" She asked. With a nod, he answered, "Well, the girls have packed everyone's clothes into the suitcases." Mum said, pointing to the cases on the floor "Scott would you load those into the trunk of the car please?"

Once this was done the six of us loaded into the car. I sat in the front seat between Mum and Dad, my three siblings filled up the back seat. We were soon underway. Waving goodbye to all of our old neighbors, who were standing on the curb sides. We drove by our old school, and then traveled further until we passed what would be our new school. We continued over a hill and, once down the other side, saw a large baseball diamond. At the corner of this ball field was a road. This was to be our new address. We turned here and followed along this side of the diamond. Where the field ended, there were swings and a slide. Behind these were two tennis courts. We drove past five more houses on each side of the road, they were all much nicer and larger than the houses on our old street.

Within just a few days, they had moved us to our new home. A beautiful, modern house that, from the street, looked like a bungalow because of the sloping lawn up to the front door. Walking through the carport to the back yard I saw that it was built on a wonderful, water front lot on an Inlet. Turning left out of the carport I could see it was actually 2 stories, with stairs up to the kitchen and patio.

The kitchen was very large with an automatic washer and dryer at one end; no more fighting with that old wringer washer for our Mum. There was a window over the sink and a larger window over the table area, both overlooking the beautiful water inlet! Across from the kitchen was a large entrance foyer. Leading to the left of the kitchen was a hallway to the bedrooms. The first door on the left was to a large bathroom, the only one, with a huge mirror and counter top. Ideal for teenage girls! At the end of the hall, next to the bathroom, was the bedroom Corinne and I would share. It was quite spacious, with a large closet and a picture window that faced the backyard and the water. Across the hall was the master bedroom and next to it a den, which would serve as Lynn's bedroom. The kitchen had 4 doors that entered it. The back door from the stairs, a basement door facing the back door, the foyer door and a sliding pocket door to the dining room. The dining room had two large windows, one that faced the neighbor's yard and a huge picture window that overlooked the patio and the water at the back. This room would be used for Scott's bedroom until the basement, which had the same floor space as the upstairs, could be finished and until we had dining room furniture.

We thought ourselves very lucky to be in such a wonderful home complete with a dishwasher and we knew it would not have been possible without Edward. I hated myself for feeling this unease with him. Already, I owed him a lot and I was determined to make my Mum happy by being nice.

Chapter 15

It was almost time for my 7th birthday. Mum asked me whom I wanted to invite to my party. I didn't know anyone in my new neighborhood yet but I really wanted to ask Darren and Cathy. Mum thought that would be okay and she wanted me to ask Linda. She was a niece to Edward that had me over to her house the previous Saturday to play. Mum felt sorry for her because she was an only child and didn't have any friends. I thought that she was weird but, if it made Mum happy, sure she could come to my birthday party.

I felt like I was at summer camp. It was fun exploring the neighborhood and setting up where my toys went in my room but it sure didn't feel like home. A few days passed by slowly and then it was my birthday party. My friends and Linda came. I was happy to show them around my new home. We played pin the tail on the donkey and had hot dogs and birthday cake. Then things felt so strange that we were almost bored with each other. Were we so different just because we were in a different place? This would become my normal feeling, disassociated and uncomfortable.

The following morning, Corinne and I, dressed in our pajamas, were eating our breakfast when Edward said, "I don't think it right for young girls to run around in their pajamas and nightgowns. The material can be too thin against burgeoning young flesh." We didn't understand this as we had always eaten our breakfast in our nightwear to keep our school clothes from getting spilled on. If our getting dressed before breakfast helped Edward feel more comfortable, then that's what we would do. Somehow, we felt more comfortable being fully dressed anyway, now.

Lynn had one-year left of high school and had to take an hour-long bus ride there and back daily. Scott was in Junior High and took a school bus for 40 minutes to near where we used to live. He was happy to do this as he went to school with all his old friends. Corinne and I walked ¾ of a mile to our elementary school, through a country subdivision. She was grade 5 and I grade 2. Mrs. Reitzma was my teacher and I fell in love with her jewelry the first day. She probably made them herself, with rocks and flowers that she collected from her travels around the world, set in clear plaster casts. Earrings and necklaces to match!

I met a girl named Donna Billingsly. She lived on the same street as I did. She introduced me to her friend, Crystal Price, who also lived on our road. We three became close friends. From that day on, we walked home together. I had so much to tell Mum all about my new school, the teacher and my friends. I changed out of my school clothes right away, put on my play clothes and went to call on Donna. Her house was also on the water. She had a sister and two brothers. Her dad was at work as a police officer and her Mum was a very nice lady. Donna showed me her Barbie dolls, which she even had made houses for out of cardboard. We played with these until it was time for me to go home for dinner.

When I went in the house everyone was home. Mum was cooking dinner. Edward and Scott were in the basement measuring for where to start building his workshop. This would be the first project. Lynn was in her room sewing her name onto her gym strip and cooking apron for school. Corinne had finished covering her textbooks in paper sleeves from grocery bags and was now watching television.

"Dinner's ready," called Mum in a voice filled with a new contentment. We all went to the kitchen, where the table was set for the six of us. Dinner was pork chops with mashed potatoes, peas and carrots. We all had things to talk about after our first day at our new schools. It seemed like an ideal family, happily chatting together, well fed, in a warm home. Maybe our Mother's wish was finally coming true.

After dinner, Mum showed Corinne and I how to pack the dirty dishes into the dishwasher and which dishes we would need to wash by hand. Corinne chose to wash the hand dishes and I would dry. When we were done, Corinne phoned one of her new friends and I went to the living room to watch TV. Scott and Lynn were already doing their homework, Scott at the kitchen table as the TV disturbed him in his temporary dining room bedroom. Mum was arranging some things in her room before bed. I was lying on my tummy on the carpeted floor watching a show when I noticed Edward standing at the kitchen doorway rubbing his back on the doorframe. "My back gets so itchy, it drives me crazy because I can't reach it," he said trying to get my attention. I had no answer for that so he added, "Do you think you could scratch it for me while you watch TV?" Yuck! I sure didn't want to but what could I say? There was no one else there to do it. He didn't wait for me to answer and instead proceeded to remove his shirt! My stomach again was filled with lead and I thought I might throw up! He was already lying on his stomach beside me and the best I could do was get up. "Right over here," he said pointing over his shoulder to where he wanted me to scratch. Dinnertime had been so nice, I didn't want to spoil that happy family feeling. Maybe this is the kind of things good families did? I began to scratch him, hating the sticky, fleshy feel of him. "Oh, that feels so much better," he purred. My nausea was worse at the realization that his dead skin cells were filling my nails. I think, somehow, I left the planet at that moment because I had no idea how long I continued my chore before my Mum appeared at the end of the hallway. She was chuckling at the sight of her little daughter playing with her new Dad. She had no idea what an ordeal it was for me. Instead, it made her happy, thinking how close her family was becoming. It went unnoticed that I left the room, as soon as she appeared, to go scrub my nails in the bathroom. This became a ritual that I avoided as much as I could until the urge finally passed him or he realized how much I hated it.

Edward focused on his business and on building his workshop in the basement. This took a few months to accomplish. The area ran the width of the house under the dining room and living room, about 12'x32'. There would be a small room, 12'x 4' for the oil tank, the main workshop, 12'x 20', and a storage room of about 12'x 8' for his painting supplies. He raised the floor above the cement on 2"x 4" s covered with plywood and linoleum. He dry-walled, painted and made a workbench along the windowed, 20' wall. His workbench would support the televisions that he would repair. He was a very hard worker and hired Scott to help him paint. Scott was paid in trade, which meant he was allowed to move his bedroom into the workshop until his actual room was built. He was happy to move out of the dining room.

Mum picked out a table for the dining room. It wasn't the table she would really like, but would do for now as there was so much money to be spent on the renovations. "This will at least give us a table to have Christmas dinner on." she said with a twinkle in her eye.

Chapter 16

That Saturday, she had a hair appointment with her hairdresser, Rose. Corinne was at her friend's, Lynn was at her new job at the jewelry store and Scott was at his friend Dennis' house working on their science project. That left me to ride around with Edward while he delivered the three televisions he had repaired that week. I always enjoyed going for long car rides and this would be really long.

By the time we were on the way to the third customer's home, I really had to go to the washroom. I was a little embarrassed to have to tell Edward this but it was either that or wet my pants. "I really have to go to the washroom." I said feeling mortified. "Oh, that's a little problem out here as there are no public washrooms. Just let me drop off this last television set, then I will drive by the Lagoon on the way to get your Mum. You could squat down behind the car and pee on the sand," said Edward. This really was true back in 1962. There were no McDonald's restaurants here on the island yet and no other public washrooms, that I knew of.

We parked in front of the house and Edward carried in the television. In just moments, he was back and we drove the block to the Lagoon. Parking parallel to the road, I got out of the back, passenger door squatted over the sand and relieved myself. Then I started to cry, realizing that there was no paper to catch the drip. "Now what?" asked Edward. "I need paper to catch the drip." I said. "We will have to use my hanky." huffed Edward as he jumped from the car and raced around to where I was squatting. He lifted me on to the back seat and fell to his knees onto the floor, shutting the car door behind him. As a loud, roar of rolling thunder hit my ears, Edward kneeled over me, split my knees apart, and patted my urethra dry with his hanky. Suddenly a blinding flash of lightning lit the sky. The rain started to fall in torrents, leaving trails on the window. My mind was racing. My insides were screaming no, oh please no! My Mummy had told me these were my private parts, nobody was ever to touch them. The look on his face left no doubt that he had never seen a little girl's private parts before. As he touched me delicately and stared with amazement he said, "This looks just like a keyhole." I suddenly felt sick to my stomach and had to look away, off into space. I concentrated on the wet trails on the window. This man was my new Daddy and it would have to be okay. I would just have to forget this whole affair. At that moment, Sarah, an alter ego, was created by my mind to protect Hanna. Sarah would remain seven years old and would remember the facts that Hanna couldn't face. Sarah remembered Edward running his figures along the lips of Hanna's vagina, remarking how much little girls looked like women only miniature. He cupped Hanna's private parts in his palm, saying "I know I shouldn't be doing this." Thankfully, he finally stopped what he was doing and we continued on to pick up Mum.

That fall, Donna and I signed up for Brownies. I enjoyed the time spent imagining we lived in a forest with a magic wishing pond. I felt like I was in the storybook about Pookie, the little rabbit that could fly. We got to wear uniforms that made us feel like we belonged. We earned badges by learning arts, crafts, cooking, sewing, how to set up camp, being kind to others, etc.

Pat would not be home for Christmas again this year and that was what really mattered to me. It was great to be with all the rest of my family, in such a wonderful home, getting great presents but it wasn't complete without Pat. My main gift this year was a crib for my doll. It was about 3'long x1.5'wide x 1.5 high and had one side that went up and down for lifting the baby in and out, just like a real crib! The doll I got onboard the ship 2 years ago, was still my favorite and always slept in that crib. (Unfortunately, a few months later, just about Easter time, I was changing my doll out of a pullover sweater when the neck was too small to get over her head. It took her head off with it! I was devastated! We could manage to fold her neck back into the head hole, but the head would not stay on. I was distraught until Mum told me that they would take her to the doll hospital to get her repaired.)

We did have a great turkey dinner with all the trimmings in our grand dining room but it all seemed flat to me without Pat. Edward raised his glass to make a toast, "Cheers to our first Christmas in our new home. Tomorrow we are all invited to my brother Cliff's home for a Boxing Day afternoon. It will give you a chance to meet some of my family." he said.

While Corinne and I did dishes, we played an Elvis Presley Christmas album. Elvis was always Pat's favorite. He emulated him with his hair cut and style of dressing. Pat also had a deep, rich voice when he sang. Now I really missed his warm, crooked smile so much like Elvis'. When Elvis sang Blue Christmas he sounded, to me, just like Pat. My tears just couldn't be held back. "Oh, come on Tink, you'll see him soon. Don't let Mum see you or you'll ruin her Christmas," warned Corinne. I didn't answer her, as there was nothing to say. I just thought to myself how I would write a letter to Pat's boss to see if he could come home for Christmas next year.

The next morning, we got up, had our breakfast, did our usual chores, then got dressed to go visiting. It was exciting to wear my good clothes two days in a row. I'm sure that Corinne felt the same way. Mum explained that there would probably be a buffet style lunch as there usually is at this type of thing. The six of us climbed into Edward's car. It felt so special to have a car to travel in and not need to catch a bus to go where we needed. This was another thing we needed to thank Edward for.

It was about a 10-minute drive to get to (Uncle) Cliff's house. It was a beautiful two-story home with four bedrooms, which they needed for their four children, three girls and a boy. The children ranged in age from 7 to 15. The youngest was a boy, Cliff junior. After the first few uncomfortable minutes of meeting everyone. Cliff junior invited me to "come down stairs to see something really neat." We went down the stairs from the kitchen to the family room. Cliff junior opened a closed door saying, "This door will be locked when the suite is finished. My Uncle Frank and his family will be living here then and they will have the key. Until then we are allowed to play in it." He opened a kitchen cupboard and showed me all of his toy cars and trucks.

Corinne, Scott and some of the older girls had gone into the other side of the family room and were taking turns playing ping-pong. Mum, Edward and Lynn remained upstairs with Cliff Senior and his wife, Brenda. Several hours passed by when we realized it must be dinner time.

"Oh, my goodness where has the time gone?" exclaimed our Mother, "We must be getting home!"

"Please have your dinner with us before you leave. Brenda has been preparing this smorgasbord for days now." piped up Uncle Cliff. "Oh, we really couldn't, as we have left our dog indoors, but thank you very much." said Mum. "Surely, he can wait just a little longer while we eat," begged Edward. "The food looks so good!" Having already grabbed a plate, he started to make his selections.

The food really did look delicious, roasted ham, turkey, lasagna and we hadn't eaten in hours. We enjoyed our scrumptious dinner, and left for home an hour later. "I hope Cocoa has his legs crossed," commented Mum as we entered the driveway. As the car came to a stop, Edward darted into the house with the rest of us close on his heels. The second that the key turned the lock, the door burst open. Cocoa darted past all of us, and relieved himself on the lawn. "Looks like we were just in time." stated Edward. "I don't know about that" said Mum "I think I smell something bad." We darted off in different directions to look. Corinne, shouting from her room, "He's been jumping on my bed. He may have been trying to get out the window." "I see what he did" complained Edward with screwed up nose, pointing under the tree. "I guess the poor dog had tried to get outside but, when he couldn't, he went where he deemed best, under a tree." There, under our Christmas tree, was a pile of poop! Worst of all he had chosen to go right on top of my chocolate animal cookies! I would never forget this boxing day.

Chapter 17

After the Christmas holiday was over, we were back-to-school. I think the part I liked best about grade two was Arithmetic. I liked how Mrs. Reitsma taught it, using bright pink plastic coffee stir sticks. She had some singles, some bundled in groups of ten or 100. It really helped to make sense of how you could carry a number over when you were subtracting. We just opened up the bundle of ten and put them on the ones side. For example, 23 minus 5. We would open one bundle of tens so we could see you actually take five away from 13 leaving 8 ones and one bundle of tens still tied up making 18. It was so magical to me and really became a game.

She read stories to us for one hour each day. This was to give us an interest in learning to read. I had been so lucky to have older siblings who had always read to me. It was hard to imagine that some kids weren't so lucky!

My grade two year passed by in a blur of disassociation. Still longing to be in a "Leave it to Beaver" household occupied my every moment. I refused to face my feelings of discomfort, not knowing how to put them into words, or how to keep them from messing up the perfect family world I so desired.

I remember one day, standing in the covered, crowded playground at school when an older boy ran into me with such force that I fell flat on my back 3' away. I landed so hard that the air was knocked out of me. I managed to pull myself to my feet by climbing the coat of a girl in my class. I tried to tell her that I couldn't breathe but there was no sound. She realized the problem and somehow managed to get me to the nurse's room. Everything was just going black when a sudden gush of air filled my lungs. It was as if a balloon popped in my throat and suddenly I was able to breathe again. This made me see how important it is to live each day as if it were your last and I chose to see everything in a more positive light from that moment forward.

I would start by trying to see my new Dad as a man who was really doing his best to be a good dad. I would try to ignore some of his annoying habits. Like when he would be shirtless and put his arms up, elbows bent straight out and his hands on his bald head saying he was pushing a button to make his muscles dance in his chest. This nauseated me. My Mother would giggle coyly at him and I felt I was intruding on an intimate affair. I would add this to my ignore list from now on.

That afternoon Dad surprised me by picking me up after school. Corinne was at home sick so it was just Dad and I together, and again I felt nervous.

"I have a good surprise for you," he explained, "Your doll is all better now and we can go and pick her up at the hospital."

I was so excited! We drove away from the school, in the direction of home. When we reached our road, he did not turn but carried straight ahead. I felt terrified and said, "Maybe you should just let me out here."

"What, you don't want to get your doll? Well, why did I bother making this special trip? If you don't want her, I'm sure they would give her to some other little girl," his voice was very strained and I was afraid that I had made him angry. Apologetically I said, "Yes, I really would like to get my doll." "That's better then," he growled.

We had driven to the stop sign at the highway, and then continued across the highway till the first driveway. Here we turned right into a very private yard. The house was encased down one side by the raised highway, and the other side by the raised train track. The backside by a raised road way and the front was hidden by a huge row of blackberry bushes. At the back of this yard stood a huge, two story house which Edward called the doll hospital. My emotions were so mixed. I was happy to be getting my doll back, but afraid of what could happen while no one else could see. Edward stopped the car next to a big dump truck that was parked in the yard. "I'll just take their TV in with me and I'll be back with your doll," Edward said.

I felt both relieved and excited. I anxiously looked around the yard while I waited for my doll. About twenty minutes later, Edward walked from the house with the doll wrapped in a blanket. He began unwrapping the doll. As he was handing it to me he grabbed my knees pulling me forward on the seat. With this he said "Now this is a good time to show you how babies are born." Placing the baby face down under my butt, he added "The Mother starts grunting and pushing out the baby like this" and he showed me with his hands moving the baby out from under me. To my dismay this wasn't even MY doll!

He drove us home after this. Mum asked where we had been. Edward answered, quite defensively, "I picked Hanna up from school to save her from having to walk home alone as I knew Corinne was already home. Then I took her to get a doll, to replace her old one that she broke the head off, and what do I get for being nice? The third degree, like I did something wrong! Remind me not to do any favors for you again!" he said nodding at me. I ate my dinner quietly, dried the dishes and excused myself to go to my room to do homework. The end of this day couldn't come soon enough.

In the following days, the construction on our basement continued. The rumpus room was done next. A 30' room along the other end of the house under my room, Corinne's room and the master bedroom. When this was completed, Scott moved his bed from the workshop into the rumpus room. His room would be finished next. In the meantime, 8' tall bamboo mats, hanging from the ceiling, divided the basement up. There was an area where we hung a dartboard and an area for Cocoa's bed and dish.

Chapter 18

Spring and summer were so beautiful that year of '63. Pat came home for his first summer visit since leaving home for training. We were all so happy to see him, with the exception of Cocoa, who bit him. Just a slight nip, enough to show Pat how much it had hurt him, when Pat left home.

Pat was driving a beautiful powder blue Beaumont, something he had always dreamed of owning. We went everywhere together for the 10 days he was home. One of the first things he wanted to do was to go clam digging at a huge beach near the airport. We had worn our oldest clothes and big gumboots. Pat always loved fresh seafood and he really had missed this being on duty in Saskatchewan. He was showing me how to dig very carefully, on a 45-degree angle, so as not to split the shells. A man came walking out from the shore and started talking to Pat. "It's good to see that you know what you are doing, not like so many white men who don't care what they destroy, they only care about how much they can get for free," said the man, then he continued, "Did you know to return the shells to the beach after you have eaten the clams?" Pat replied that he didn't know this. "Oh yes, the shells get broken down over time and become part of the new sand," the man explained, "This is Indian land and we do not mind sharing all of its riches with everyone, as long as people care for the land and help it to remain bountiful." Pat thanked the man for the information, and for helping us fill our big turkey roaster, full of clams. We enjoyed the long ride home in Pat's slick car.

The clams were put in cold, fresh running water to make them spit out any sand they were holding. Then they went straight onto the stove burner to steam with the lid on for a few minutes until the clams opened their shells to show they were dead and ready to eat. Things couldn't have been better! Those clams were excellent right out of the shells, no need for butter or garlic. Mum complained a bit about the smell in her kitchen but it was soon gone with the window and door open. We showed Pat the model family he had hoped for, hiding the fact that I still felt like I was living in a place belonging to somebody else, and how uncomfortable I was with Edward. I couldn't tell Pat.

One of the days we went for a hike on the mountain. It took us just about the whole day. Lynn, Scott and Corinne had come along as well and it was great for us all to be together! We rested in a beautiful meadow, in the shade of some mighty oak trees. We all marched upward at our own speed. Sometimes I would be with Corinne, then walking with Lynn and Scott and sometimes I even got a piggyback from Pat or Scott. By the time we reached the top, we were all content to sit and enjoy the beautiful view. One side overlooked the blue waters of the Inlet, the other a sea of green trees heading south towards downtown.

Early one morning Pat and Scott went to a Marina and rented a boat for a few hours to go fishing. They each caught 2 or 3 salmon, which would be our dinner that night! In the afternoon, I had been playing at Donna's house and decided to go see if Pat and Scott were still in our driveway, tuning up the Beaumont. Donna rode her bike over and I ran along beside her.

"Where did you ladies come from, and I don't believe that we've met before?" said Pat saluting to Donna.

"Oh, this is my friend Donna that I wrote to you about." I explained.

"Well it's a pleasure to meet you Donna," he offered and then asked me, "and where is your bike, Tink?"

"I usually ride Corinne's 3 speed bike but she has it today," I told him as I suggested to Donna, "Let's go to the park." And away I ran and Donna rode. We had a great meal of barbequed salmon with potato salad, green salad and corn on the cob for dinner that night.

Another day was spent hiking around the Lake and going for root beer and a hamburger at A&W after. After that, Pat went to meet up with some of his old friends. He didn't get home that night until well after I was in bed. In the morning, Lynn told me that Pat had come in laughing and went running into Mum's room and jumped on her bed, making it fall to the floor! Mum and Dad were in the bed at the time but were not angry.

Pat unfortunately was very hard on himself. He fixed the bed right away and apologized profusely.

It had been great having Pat at home again. I had felt at ease, myself, during this time. Then his holiday was over and Pat had to drive back to a little town in Saskatchewan, which was his first posting. It was three days' drive away. Saying good-bye never got any easier!

Chapter 19

The rest of the summer passed with days filled with playing Barbie's, going to the park at the corner of our road, playing in the empty lot next to Donna's, and listening for the ice cream truck to come by. It was an unusual looking truck with music playing to attract the kids. I remember it going by at our old house but we could never afford to get an ice cream then. This was another positive way that Edward had sweetened my life. Now, when I heard the ice cream truck's music, I could run and get a treat!

We had built a nice little play- house in the lot. I had carried over my little ironing board, my doll stroller, a plastic tub to use as a sink, a Japanese orange wooden box filled with dishes to nail up on the tree to use as a cupboard and I even had my Grandmother's old kitchen clock, that didn't work anymore but we could pretend. I was just standing on an overturned bucket to reach to put the clock on the top of the cupboard, when I heard the ice cream truck! I was so excited that I lost my balance, fell from the bucket, knocked the clock flying into the muddy boggy stream by the lot and then followed it myself! The muck smelled putrid and felt about the same; cold, clammy and sticky. Donna was running to my rescue already because of the scream I had emitted as I fell.

"Oh, Hanna!" she gasped as she saw me. I was trying to pull myself out of the sickening mud without vomiting, which was no easy endeavor. Donna held out her hand to me to pull me back to shore. I began to cry, more because I had lost my Grandmother's clock than for anything else. As soon as I was on shore Donna and I both headed for home to clean up. I thought that my Mum would be angry at me for losing her Mother's clock. I also thought she wouldn't let me go back to Donna's because we had played so close to the water. She wasn't mad at all, just wanted me to get right in the tub and wash my hair. How could I be so wrong about how my Mum would feel? I was very confused.

The following morning, I awoke, dressed and went to the kitchen to get my bowl of "Alphabet's" cereal. While I was eating, the doorbell rang and Mum went to answer it. I heard her talking to a man who I assumed was a customer of Dad's. "Come and look at this, Hanna. You won't believe it!" cheered my Mum. I ran down from the table and into the foyer. There, just inside the door was a huge box! It was larger than the box Mum's pots and pans had come in from Pat. "What is it?" I asked. "Well, I don't know but it has your name on it," Mum answered. I was almost afraid to approach the box. "Did you order something?" asked Scott as he came up from downstairs to see what the excitement was about. "No, I don't have any money to order anything," I replied. "Well, you'd better open it or you'll never know what it is," instructed Mum.

My interest was suddenly aroused as I remembered that tomorrow was my birthday! I started pulling at the brown parcel tape that held it shut. It peeled away easily releasing the lid. I quickly pulled the top opened and peered inside to see shining chrome. "It's a bike!" I screamed. I started reaching down into the box to pull it out when I heard Scott chuckling, "I'll help you get it out, Tink" We laid the box on its side and slid the bike out of the top. It was so beautiful! Shiny chrome handle bars with white plastic handle grips, a blue metal frame with a black leather seat and black pedals. White fenders finished it off. "This is so beautiful, is it really mine?" I asked.

Scott turned the empty box upside down and out fell a card with my name on it. I scrambled to reach it and see who would have given me this bike. Inside the envelope was a card that said, "To my little sister". It had a picture of a woodland stream on it and it made me think of when Pat taught me the poem of "Fishy, fishy, in the brook. Daddy, catch him on a hook. Mummy fry him in the pan, for a very little man." I would never have thought that Pat could afford to buy me this bike. Inside the card, he had written, "To Tinkerbell, now you won't have to run after your friend Donna again!" I started to cry thinking how special this was of Pat to give me a bike and how much I missed him. "This is no time to cry! Don't you want to ride your new bike?" asked Scott a little bewildered. In a few moments, I was soaring by houses on my new wheels! I loved that bike almost as much as I loved the brother who gave it to me!

The next day was my eighth birthday and the plan was to have Donna over for dinner, go to the astrophysical observatory to look at the stars and then have a sleep over. It was a wonderful way to turn eight, except that Edward walked in on Donna and I when we were changing for bed. I felt sick in my tummy as if Edward had planned to see both Donna and I nude, and he would enjoy it.

Scott continued working on antennae jobs and frugally banked his money over this time. He made a few friends in the neighborhood and, at 15, he had enough money to buy an older car that he and his friends fixed up. All of Corinne's girlfriends raved about how handsome Scott was! "He looks just like that cute guy who plays Dr. Stone's son on the Donna Reid Show", cooed one of the girls holding one hand clenched at her mouth and her other hand to her chest. She was closing her eyes as if it was too much to bear. Until he was old enough to get his license, Scott used to just drive across our road onto a dirt path that wound through the bush behind the park. He would let me ride with him and I loved it!

Lynn had grown in to a very beautiful young lady with long, dark blonde hair and a cute figure. She was popular, with a number of young men courting her. They often would take her kid sister along on dates, lucky me! I was a good escort, with them on a drive for an ice cream or to the fair. She started to receive bouquets of flowers from one of her beaus, Michael and, within a few months, they were engaged! The wedding was planned for Nov. of next year, 1964.

Chapter 20

A final family vacation was scheduled to happen before the wedding. During the summer break from school, the summer I turned 9 years old, the 6 of us were to drive to Saskatchewan to visit Pat! This was no easy task. It required us to drive about 8-10 hours per day for 3-4 days to get there. Then have 6-8 days with Pat and drive 3-4 days back, including a 95-minute ferry trip each way.

Mum and Edward had the front seat to themselves. Lynn, Corinne and Scott shared the back seat and I had the back of the station wagon to share with all of our camping equipment and luggage. Things started out not too badly. We were all up at 5:30 A.M. hoping to make the 7A.M. ferry, which was a 45-min drive from our home. The excitement of the trip had my stomach feeling queasy. Mum asked me to go to the basement to feed Cocoa. As soon as the cooler air of the basement touched my face, I vomited. Now there was a mess to clean up.

We missed the 7am ferry and were just lucky to make the 8. I loved going on the boat. We had our breakfast onboard and each got a book to entertain us. I chose an "Archie" comic as I had never had one before. It was very special to me. We drove for hours after leaving the ferry. The weather was extremely warm and there was a lot of road construction going on. We were stopped in a mile, long line-up while they were blasting. It was 2 hours before we could move at all.

Finally, creeping along, we reached a town in the mountains where we decided to go to a restaurant for lunch. Being as I was sitting on our bedding in the station wagon, I had to take my shoes off and because they each had two buckles on them, it became a standing joke that we lost 20 miles every time Hanna had to put her shoes on! We had never eaten at a restaurant before! Edward was very anxious to get on the road again after we ate. He thought we were way behind. After using the washroom, we were underway again. I played with my cut-out dolls for hours until it was too dark to see.

"We should have stopped at that last campsite," snapped my Mother's voice with fatigue.

"Just settle down, there will be somewhere we can stop soon. We have to make better time tomorrow or we won't be able to make it to Pat and back in 2 weeks," answered Edward obviously quite annoyed. I lay down on the blankets now and tried to cover myself with some. I could hear them nattering at each other while I drifted off to sleep.

"Well, this won't be big enough for all of us," I woke to hear my Mother saying. I raised my sleepy head and saw Scott laughing at me. "Aren't you a sight Tink! They are just checking out this little motel for us for tonight. It's so late and it's too dark to get a campsite now," Scott explained to me. Edward, Mum, Lynn and Corinne had gone into the little cabin, which contained 2 double beds and a tiny bathroom. We were way up in the Rocky Mountains and the cabins seemed so quaint. "Lynn and Corinne can share that bed, Scott and Hanna can sleep in the car," announced Edward. "It's too cold for them to sleep out there," shouted our Mother's voice, stressed and fatigued by the long day of travelling. Edward appeared at the door to the cabin. He walked towards the car, zipping his coat as he came he said, "You guys will be okay sleeping in the car, right? Scott can have the back and Hanna can fit on the back seat." "Sure, we'll be fine," assured Scott. "It is cold enough to snow out here tonight," shivered Edward, "but you have lots of blankets, right?" With this said he strolled back to the cabin sending us a "Goodnight" through the frosty air.

I was very tired that night and didn't remember falling asleep. I awoke to Scott putting another blanket on me. "Good morning Tink. Are you cold? I'm going to go in and ask Edward if I can have the key to start the car warming so you can get dressed," Scott explained. I wasn't awake enough to know where I was or if I was cold. Then I felt afraid when I realized that I couldn't see out the car window, was I going blind? Scott laughed again at me when he saw my fear and knew why. "Oh, you silly! The windows are frosted over with ice. That's why you can't see through them, there's nothing wrong with your eyes," he chuckled as he climbed out of the car.

I snuggled tighter into my covers when the icy air from outside touched me. My clothes were still on from yesterday as I was too tired last night to change into my pajamas. Scott was back with the keys now and proudly started the car as if it were his own. In just a few moments, it was warm enough to climb out of my cocoon. Mum called us into the cabin where we could take turns washing our faces and eat our cereal, not in bowls like at home, but right out of individual boxes with the milk poured right into them.

We were ready in a flash and on the road again. Coming down from the beautiful mountains I was amazed by the vista before us! The land fell smooth and flat! No more big trees and mountains. Instead, rolling hills and grasses as far as you could see! For miles and miles, it was the same. I stared out the back window at the wall of beautiful mountains that seemed to end abruptly.

I turned to see out the front window and like the scene in "The Wizard of Oz", looking across the field of grasses stood tall buildings. It seemed so unreal to be driving by miles and miles of grass and suddenly to be in a big city. We stopped for an hour or so to shop. I got a white cowboy hat and teddy bear for my 9th birthday. Corinne was embarrassed because I was too old for teddy bears. The feeling we got from this big city was that it went on for miles, as if they had so much land they didn't need to keep the city in any order. We had soon had enough and decided to look for a campsite.

It was 3 o'clock and we were getting pretty hungry for the lunch we had skipped. While driving, we each had an apple to tie us over. An hour out of the city, we came upon a "Campground ½ mile" sign. We wondered how this could be as we were still driving through nothing but fields of grass and then we saw it! Dust roads etched in a grassy field with one, four foot, spindly, year old tree planted beside each picnic bench! Two outhouses stood between every third and fourth campsite. "Welcome to camping in Alberta," laughed Scott. "Well it will do for overnight. We can have a picnic lunch, set up camp, have an easy dinner and an early night so we can get to Pat by lunch time tomorrow," stated Mum to be sure there would be no discussion.

Edward and Scott got right at setting up the tent. Corinne and Lynn went for water at the pump while Mum searched through the cooler for sandwich goodies and I set the table. In a few moments, it actually looked more like a campsite and we were all busily eating our picnic of cheese and crackers with pickles. The little tree offered no shade from the searing sun, which would be setting in just an hour or two. The kettle was just coming to the boil offering solace to our Mum. We even had tea with the adults today. Mine was still ½ milk and a teaspoon of sugar, but it made me feel relaxed and grown up.

After lunch Scott, Corinne and I started throwing around a soft ball. Edward came over to join us. I know I should have been very happy. How many kids have their Dad play ball with them? There was just something about Edward that made me uncomfortable. Right away the game changed from just catch to, almost, touch football. He would run too far to catch the ball, bumping into Corinne or I each time. He would chuckle about it being a clumsy accident but after the second time it lost the humor. I felt so guilty. Why couldn't I just enjoy the game? Instead I just said, "I don't want to play anymore." "Oh, getting too tough for you then?" snickered Edward. I hated him for that. I didn't want to hurt his feelings but I didn't think he should make fun of me because he couldn't play right. "Forget about it", I thought, "Just go play with your cut-outs". The game of catch broke up. Corinne went to read her magazine, Scott went to throw rocks at some fence posts and I didn't notice where Edward went.

Soon I smelled hamburgers cooking over a little campfire. We had the best hamburgers out in the sunset that night. We washed the dishes in a plastic bin, that we later used to wash our faces in. It was so quiet here when there was no traffic on the highway, which was only 50 or 60 feet away. The sky felt like it sat on your shoulders with no mountains to hold it up and there seemed to be more stars in it than I had ever seen before!

The plan was for Mum, Edward, Lynn and Corinne to share the tent, Scott and I to share the car again. I went in the tent first to change into my pajamas. Lynn and Corinne were already in there making their beds. As I was changing Edward came in for something. I was so embarrassed that he saw me undressed! Corinne saw me grab a blanket to hide behind. "Oh, Tink, don't be embarrassed, there's nothing to see yet, at 9," she whispered to me. Edward left the tent and I scrambled into my pajamas, afraid that he would come back. I gathered my clothes and went outside to brush my teeth, still blushing. Soon I was a bed on the back seat of the car under just a sheet, as it was so warm here compared to how it had been in the mountains. I had trouble sleeping for feeling ashamed. I tried not to think about it and concentrate only on seeing Pat tomorrow! The morning was a long time in coming.

 Chapter 21

The bright sunlight and traffic noise woke me. I sat up and saw Scott outside walking back from the outhouse. I stepped out of the door and headed in the direction that Scott had come from. "Good morning, Tink, are you getting up already, it's only 6:30," he greeted me.

"I can't wait to see, Pat," was my answer as I passed him. Returning to the car I passed Lynn and Mum on their way to the outhouses. "Good, we are all up. I guess none of us can wait to see Pat. We'll have our cereal and get packed up to go," said Mum.

I dressed under the sheet on the back seat of the car. It wasn't easy, but I didn't want to change in that tent again. When I was done dressing, and had folded up my bedding, I got out of the car to the smell of coffee perking. Edward always had coffee in the morning before noon and only tea after that. An hour or two later we were on the road headed east to Saskatchewan.

We needed the windows down already, the day was so hot. Edward was driving fast on this straight, boring road, as did everyone else. When a car passed us, going in the opposite direction, our car was shaken by the suction created, causing a jet sound and a rocking motion lasting a few seconds each time. Looking at the map Lynn said, "It looks like about 370 miles to the border between Alberta and Saskatchewan and then another 200 miles to where Pat lives. I think it will be about 2 o'clock when we get there." "That's not counting the bathroom stops along the way, and how long it takes Tink to put on her shoes," chuckled Scott.

"We won't be doing this trip again so enjoy the scenery and we'll get there when we get there," answered Mum. She and Edward chatted on while Lynn and Corinne read their books, Scott adjusted himself to lie back with his feet out the window and I started coloring in my "Flintstone" coloring book.

Hours passed, as did the fields of grains, when finally, Edward announced, "Here's the border." I looked up just in time to see a large sign that said, "Leaving Alberta" with a pink wild rose painted on it. In passing it, I could see the other side of it said "Leaving Saskatchewan" and had an orange trillium painted on it.

"Good, now we'll look for somewhere we can stop for a picnic lunch and a cup of tea," said Mum looking at Edward as if for agreement. "Sure, that sounds good to me," was his response. In another hour, we spotted a little watering hole with a grove of trees beside it and a few picnic tables. Soon the kettle was on the boil and salmon sandwiches were made for lunch.

"It looks like about another 80 miles before we turn off of this highway and then only about 24 miles on the smaller highway until we're there," informed Lynn checking the map. "How long is that to drive," I asked, hoping the answer wouldn't be long. "About an hour and a quarter," answered Scott. The thought of being so close to Pat was thrilling but we enjoyed our picnic outside in the hot sunlight and fresh air before piling back into the crowded station wagon.

On the road again, the scenery was much the same. Fields and fields of grain, grain elevators with the town name painted on it, and the train tracks always accompanying the highway. I heard Scott say, "We're here," and it broke me out of my trance from the repetition. I don't know what we had expected, but there was nothing here. Just more fields, a small store for groceries, a gas station out front, and an old mobile home beside the railroad tracks.

"Well, I'll go in and ask at the store. They must know where to find Pat," offered Edward.

"I'll go with you," said Scott. Inside they found a complete grocery, pharmacy, and post office only in miniature. There was just one counter with a cash register on it but no one there. "Hello, anyone here," asked Edward. "Sure, I'll be right with you," came a voice from the back room. "Good afternoon. Can I help you?" asked the man belonging to the voice, as he appeared around the corner. "Yes, we're looking for your police station," answered Edward.

"Do you need the police? Our town isn't big enough for a detachment but we can get a Constable for you if you need one?" the shopkeeper replied rather quickly. "No, no. We don't need the police. We've come to visit my wife's son," Edward responded, hoping to calm the situation.

"Oh, you must be Mr. Rutherford. It's a pleasure to meet you!" said the shop owner extending his hand. "Well, it's Mr. Brownwell, but thanks just the same," Edward said as he offered his hand. "Let me call for Pat" the shop- keeper said as he reached for the radio. "He's so excited that you folks were coming he's told us all about it! Grocery calling Constable Rutherford. Grocery calling Constable Rutherford, do you copy?" "Constable Rutherford calling Grocery. Constable Rutherford calling Grocery. Come back now." "Your folks are here now, Pat" The shopkeeper was so excited; he forgot the rules of talking on the radio. "That's good news, Glenn. Ask them to wait right there, I'll be there in 10. Constable Rutherford over and out."

Scott's face was just beaming, having heard his brother's voice sounding so official over the radio. He ran outside to tell the rest of the family all about it. Having heard Pat would be here in 10 minutes, Lynn and Corinne both ran to the gas station's washroom with their brushes in hand. I started putting my shoes on in hopes of riding with Pat in his car. I was just doing up the last buckle when I saw the police car. We were all so proud to see Pat driving it! Mum was wiping back tears when she asked, "Where do you live?" "I rent a room in a very nice farm house about 8 miles east of town," Pat answered, pointing in the direction of the house. "You will be able to rent this mobile home," he pointed to the one near the train tracks, "to stay in cheap, thanks to the owners who are away while you are here. It was either that or your tent as there is no hotel in town. I'll let you in there so you can get set up, while I finish my shift until 6P.M. Then we'll go for a drive so I can show you all the land that I patrol. It's so good to have you guys here!"

He walked across the road to the trailer, unlocked the door saying, "The owners are really nice people and want you to make yourselves at home. They changed all of the sheets so you would be comfortable. I've got to run. See you later."

I was a little disappointed that Pat wasn't wearing his red coat, leather, high top boots, and Stetson hat. Mum explained that they were only for dress, not for every day. We went inside the mobile home and found that it had 3 bedrooms. One for Mum and Edward, one with bunk beds for Corinne and I, and the third for Lynn, Scott would have the couch in the living room.

"Lynn, would you run a bath for Hanna? We'll take turns getting cleaned up so we're fresh for dinner. Scott, would you bring in the coolers first so we can get them emptied into the fridge as the ice is almost melted away. Corinne, could you bring in the clothing bags. We might as well get organized as we'll be here for 6 days or so," ordered Mum.

I went to get undressed to have my bath so everyone else could get their turns. "Yikes!" I screamed, "the water's dirty and it stinks!" Mum came running hearing my scream, "Oh, that's just because of the Sulphur here in their soil. It won't hurt you and you do need a bath," she explained. "I can't get in that," I argued unusually defiant. "Oh, all right. Scott, could you go to the store and see if they have any bubble bath?" requested Mum.

Scott went while we emptied the tub. He returned with a bottle of "Soakies". It was a bottle shaped like "Rocky" the squirrel from the cartoon "Rocky and Bullwinkle", complete with the aviator helmet and glasses. The directions said to add one capful to a bath. That amount did nothing in this dreadful water, it didn't even bubble. We continued adding capfuls until the tub had a slight haze of bubbles on it and the smell was bearable, the bottle was empty! I bathed and washed my hair in record time. Over the time we were there, I acquired quite a collection of "Soakie" bottles, including one of "Bullwinkle" with his big antlers, one of "Boris" and one of "Natasha".

After dinner, we drove for miles to see Pat's patrol area. "It's a lot of land to cover, but is there much to do other than catching speeders and assisting at accidents?" asked Edward. "You'd be surprised. Yes, the highway keeps us the busiest but last week I was investigating a robbery in one of the towns." A chorus of "What was stolen?" rang out. "Nothing big, just a television, stereo and a wheelbarrow. I just went around asking a few questions and pretty soon I knew who had done it." "How did you know? Did they confess? Did you find the stuff?" Everyone was eager to know. Pat grinned and said, "Not exactly. One man was very interested in knowing what would happen to the guy when we caught him. This was almost an admission of guilt. So, I just suggested that it would be advisable that the guilty person should turn himself in and would receive a far lesser penalty. Then he confessed and turned over the stolen items."

We all chuckled knowing that Pat would have been good at this job, as he was so righteous that he could make anyone feel guilty enough to confess. It was well passed dark at this point and the plan was for us to join Pat tomorrow on his patrol to the Hutterites commune. They had asked him to invite his family to come along. They were very proud people and wanted to show us their farm and huge pig barns.

Chapter 22

We were driving over miles of farmland, following the police car with Pat and Lynn in it. Pat could only have one ride along (a guest) with him at a time so we would have to take turns. It turned out to be a very interesting day.

The farm was many hectares large with about 8 buildings and 2 massive L-shaped barns. The Hutterites are a religious group originally from Russia. They live by strict rules and they share all of the work on schedules. One week a woman would be on baking duty where she and others would start before dawn making bread to be baked in their huge commercial ovens. The oven racks rotated, with 6 loaves on each tier and 20 tiers! This would be enough bread for the whole commune for a few days. Then they would make buns, pies, cookies, etc. for both the family and for sale. The next week she could be on laundry duty. They had a laundry similar to that of a hospital, only on a smaller scale. These women would also do any mending of the groups clothing, sheets, towels, etc. Another week she could be on child minding duty whereas the men were strictly on farming duties: ploughing fields, feeding pigs, milking cows, etc.

We were amazed by the large dining hall with long tables enough for all 72 members, 8 families each with between 4 and 12 children! The couples each had their own bedrooms with an adjoining room for any infants. The other children shared dormitories. One for the boys/ unmarried men and one for the girls/ unmarried women.

After viewing how they lived we were treated to their pig barns. I had been in only a few barns until this time, but nothing like this! These barns were at least 1000 feet long by 40 feet wide! They did not have dirt floors, like the barns I was used to, but scrubbed concrete. Each family of pigs was corralled by a fence in an area about 10'x10'. There was no sign of dirt but the smell burned your nostrils! The Hutterites were so proud, they insisted on walking us the full length of the barn to show us all of their 900-1000 pigs!

Once outside the barns we thanked them whole-heartedly for sharing their lives with us so willingly. Complete strangers except for our brother, who they were so impressed by that they wanted to meet his family. We had really enjoyed our visit but now couldn't get back to our accommodations fast enough to get in the shower and change our clothes! It was Scott's turn to ride back in the police car with Pat. All the windows were open wide in the station wagon and still it was hard to breath. It still took a full bottle of Soakies to get me in that terrible water but I was much more determined to get in this time.

We had a great meal of barbequed chicken, boiled corn on the cob, and potato salad outside on whatever we could find to sit on. It was a beautiful prairie evening, finally cooling down from the day, the sky so clear, the air so still and my family all around! This special time came abruptly to an end, when Pat excused himself to have an early night. He was to work a 12-hour day tomorrow from 6-6. Corinne and I did the dishes outdoors that night, Lynn went to write a letter to Michael, Scott went looking for gopher holes, Mum and Edward had retired to their bed.

The next morning began hot. We were hoping to sleep in, but it was too hot to sleep. After we ate our little cereal boxes a huge train started to appear on the horizon. On the island where we lived the trains would maybe have 4 or 5 cars, this train seemed to be never ending! It began with 5 engines and Corinne began counting the cars as it rolled passed our trailer. I found a magnet, hung it on a string and went around collecting bottle caps that were all around the dirt roads near the store. The hours went by slowly in the heat. We played games of snakes and ladders, checkers, clock and I tried to color but the crayons were too soft in the heat. I continued hunting for bottle caps, collecting in total 250. We wondered if Corinne would count as many train cars as it was still passing by at 3 P.M. and the count was 185 cars.

Scott and Edward began playing catch while Mum and I peeled potatoes and carrots to cook for dinner. We would have dinner ready when Pat came home at 6. It was too hot in the trailer to cook so we set up our camp stove and cooked outside. We made pan- fried pork chops and mashed potatoes with peas and carrots. Three cabooses went by at 5:40 bringing the total cars to 279! Lynn came announcing, "See what I made." I turned to see that she had taken my bottle caps and spelled out the word Michael with them in the dirt! Oh well, what was I going to do with them anyway.

Pat arrived from his work day looking sullen and flushed. "Are you feeling okay, Pat," asked Mum. "It was just a bad day, something I can't talk about," was all Pat would say.

We all ate outdoors again hoping for a cooling breeze, which never came. We told about the huge train and the bottle caps but the air seemed filled with Pat's unease. He ate very little and asked to lie down in the trailer for a while. We looked at each other feeling cheated at losing time with him. Lynn suggested we, Scott, Corinne and I go for a walk to give him some quiet. Mum and Edward talked quietly while doing the dishes outside.

Mum was very concerned and when she heard Pat crying it was more than she could bear on the sidelines. She went quietly to him and said, "Son, surely if you talked about it, that would help." "We're not really supposed to speak about our cases to persons outside the force," he replied trying to get himself under control. "Surely if you don't tell me their names it won't hurt anyone and it could make you feel much better," she offered.

Pat wished that he could be stronger, but he really needed to tell someone this awful tale. That morning he had been ordered, in a child custody case, to seize a little five-year-old girl who had been put up for adoption at birth. She had been adopted by a wonderful family and had spent the past five years with this family. She had become the youngest daughter of two wonderful parents with a 9-year-old brother and 7-year-old sister. Recently, the birth Mother had decided that she had made a mistake in giving up her child and wanted her back. This could not be done today but in 1964 the birth Mother still had the right to her child. Pat arrived at the farm home that morning, much to his chagrin, and tried to explain the situation. The adoptive parents were appalled, horrified and tried to understand how the law could do this to their little girl, who had never known any other family. The little girl was hysterical as were her brother and sister. The parents were sobbing, as was Pat. This was a horrible situation to have to be in but it was the law at that time. Mum cried and held Pat for many moments but there was nothing anyone could do. To the day he died, Pat wondered what became of that little girl. He always felt that the Mother would want to give her back when she realized what a mess she had caused but he was never to know.

Chapter 23

The next morning Pat had a full shift of work again but he had gotten some tourist information for us on an old sod farmhouse that was about an hour drive away. We had our breakfast, packed a picnic lunch of sandwiches, watermelon, pop, tea and cookies. By 11 A.M. we were on the road for the sod house. We didn't really know what that was, but it was worth going to see, rather than waiting around the trailer again. Again, the countryside was flat with a view for miles of tall grasses. The windows were all open for the "poor man's air conditioning".

55 minutes later we were at the sod farmhouse. It actually was built of sod, turf, just like how people get their lawns rolled out today. The early settlers cut out squares of the grasses with about 2" worth of soil attached in the roots to build their houses from. There weren't many trees on the prairie and the soil worked as insulation. The house was very small, only 8'x10' and 6 1/2' tall. There was a small fireplace, for them to do their cooking in, with a metal pipe chimney. The tour guide working at the sod house told us how hard it was to survive the bitter winters on the prairie and how hard the people had to work to prepare for the rest of the year. It was very interesting and made me realize how lucky we are. It was already 2:15 when we left the sod house, with handfuls of wheat grain the guide had given us to try chewing like gum as the settlers had. It took quite a bit of chewing to get into a gummy paste and then it lacked the sweet taste of gum that we were used to. The tour guide had also told us of a small lake with picnic tables further down the road, so we were headed there now for our picnic lunch.

The road here was dusty and the air so hot it burned to breath. Thank goodness, we reached the lake just 10 minutes down the road. There was a row of poplar trees planted next to the picnic table but the shade from the trees was falling on the opposite side, so we spread a blanket from the car on the shady grass to sit and eat our lunch. The sandwiches were cheese with lettuce and tomato. It was hot enough that the cheese was a little soft and the tomato was juicy enough to wet your throat to swallow. The watermelon was the winner! It was thirst quenching and so much fun spitting seeds at my brother and sisters. It used up all of our pent-up energy from riding in the car. My hands were sticky from the watermelon juice that was also all over my shirt. I walked to the lake's edge to wash what I could. The water wasn't cold like the lake water at home but was almost bath temperature.

As I was washing my shirt and hands Scott came to join me. "Oh, look out, Tink. That black, wiggly worm in the water is a leach," he warned. "What's a leach," I asked? "Well, it's kind of a worm that sucks out other creature's blood," he explained. "Oo, people's too?"

"Yes, we have them at home too, in some lakes, and they get on people and they are hard to get off. You have to turn them just the right way or sprinkle salt on them," Scott continued. That was enough for me never to want to go swimming again!

We headed back to our blanket in the shade for some cookies and pop before the hour-long drive back. Mum was, as always having her cup of tea. We left feeling refreshed. Mum was talking about barbequing hamburgers for dinner when WHAM!! Something had darted out of a field onto the road and we had run over it! It was only seconds before we realized the terrible truth that we had hit a skunk!! Oh, the horrendous smell!! Edward quickly pulled over into the field, as some of us were about to vomit! All the doors of the station wagon flew open the second that it stopped! I rolled over the back seat and out the side door, as I couldn't wait until someone unlocked the rear door. Most of us lost our lunch and, standing holding our noses, wondered how we could get back into that car to get to a car wash.

"Well, there's no two ways about it. We have to get in and bear it until we get to a car wash. Surely the wind will blow most of it away," pondered Edward disgustedly. "I wonder where the nearest car wash would be? There isn't one in town. We'll just have to drive until we see someone to ask."

That is just what we did, very uncomfortably. It wasn't until town that we could stop to ask someone. Again, we all piled out of the car and quickly moved away from it. Edward found out that the nearest car wash was 60 miles away or, there was a hose outside the trailer he could use. Scott and Edward filled a bucket with warm soapy water and started the sickening job of trying to wash the stench away! After washing the whole vehicle once and not noticing much difference in the smell, they renewed the bucket of hot soapy water adding a bottle of lemon juice to see if it would cut the smell. After rewashing the car again, it was somewhat better, although Edward had to park the car a block away before you couldn't smell it.

He was just walking back to the trailer as Pat came home from work. Laughing Pat said, "I see you've had your first run in with a skunk!" "Scott and I washed it twice, once even with lemon but it still reeks," muttered Edward. "Yeah, there's a fortune to be made for the man who invents a soap that will remove skunk spray smell," chuckled Pat.

"Dinner's ready, come and help yourselves," called Mum. "That's music to my ears. I will sure miss that when you guys go home," sighed Pat. I suddenly had a wave of homesickness. Not for home itself, but because I hadn't thought that we would be leaving Pat here when we left for home! Pat saw the look on my face instantly and asked, "What's the matter, Tink?" I couldn't think how to put it into words, at least not without crying. "She just doesn't want to leave Pat behind," teased Corinne. She knew me too well and didn't think too highly of me.

"Oh, come on, Tink, we've got two more days yet," chuckled Pat as he gave me a little hug. "Tomorrow I don't have to go into work so we can spend the whole day together. In fact, I have a lady friend that I would like you all to meet. Her name is Veronica. She is an elementary school teacher in a nearby town. We can all drive there tomorrow to get her and then carry on to a little town I go to once a week for drinking water. We can pack a picnic, some soft balls, gloves and a bat and have a good day."

The rest of the evening went by in a flash and soon we were packing our picnic. Corinne and I both rode with Pat in his own blue Beaumont. He asked about our new house, school, friends, extra-curricular activities we were in etc. Before we knew it, we had arrived at Veronica's. "All right little ladies. I'll just go in and get her while you two gals hop in the back seat," he informed us as the car stopped in front of a small 4-plex.

I turned to make sure that Mum's car was with us. They had parked a good half block away so as not to knock Veronica out with the skunk smell. Scott had had his feet out the window while they were driving but, with the car stopped, every window was rolled up tight against the smell.

Here came Pat and Veronica holding hands. She was a pretty, slim lady with short, brown hair. She was wearing pedal pushers, that were all the rage then, and a cute cotton summer top. Pat was taking her to the station wagon to introduce her when Edward rolled down the window and shouted, "You might want to do the introductions later, away from the car."

Pat explained the situation to Veronica, they both laughed and shook their heads in agreement.

Our introductions done quickly, we had a pleasant conversation all the way to the picnic area. Veronica was very nice, in fact I felt that I should call her Miss Bloom as she seemed so much like a teacher.

Pat took out two large plastic drums that he filled with water from the pump. These two would last him for about 10 days for making lemonade, tea, brushing his teeth and drinking water. I could never have imagined driving to get drinkable water, not having lived my entire life in B.C.

Once the water drums were filled, we found a large field with poplar trees planted around the circumference. In the center were picnic tables with barbeque pits beside them. We quickly got into a fun game of softball. Mum didn't play so we were split into two teams of three players each. I was an extra player on whichever team was out to field. We had a lot of fun during our first game, which ended in a tie. We were all ready for a break and enjoyed our picnic in the shade of the poplar trees. This gave Mum and Edward a chance to get to know Veronica.

When we had finished our salmon sandwiches and celery sticks stuffed with cheese whiz, we had another refreshing watermelon and another seed fight. Mum was so embarrassed that we would do this in front of Veronica, until she joined in the fun too. She had grown up with three brothers and had obviously held her own.

We began another game of softball. We were having such a great time but was I the only one bothered by how often Edward was bumping into Veronica? He was actually hugging her to tag her out at first base! Everyone was having so much fun so I tried to let go of it. The second game drew to an end without a winner. We were all just too tired to care and Mum had lemonade and tea ready. Veronica had brought a nice surprise for all of us, a delicious orange cake with orange frosting. We enjoyed it in the shade as dusk fell.

I couldn't believe how fast the day had gone. It was time to head back and drop Veronica home. She said good-bye to all of us, adding that she hoped to see us again. Pat took her to the back door of the 4-plex. I wondered if he kissed her good-bye? Then I felt that lead feeling in my stomach again. Perhaps I was afraid that she would replace me in Pat's life? I felt the tears filling my eyes as I thought of going home without my big brother. I lay back in my seat pretending to sleep. It would be too painful to admit my feelings.

Pat and Corinne chatted on about many things, including Edward. Pat asked many questions: did Corinne think he was good to Mum? did Scott still work with him? how were the wedding plans coming for Lynn and Michael? what was he like? It seemed very soon, as I had fallen asleep, and we were at the trailer again. Just time to say good-night and we would see Pat at dinner tomorrow. We would stay at the trailer for the day getting our laundry washed, coolers refilled, car arranged, etc. for the trip home the next morning.

Chapter 24

The next day dragged by painfully. My heart ached from the weight of saying good-bye to Pat again for who knew how long? Corinne tried teasing me about it all day. I know she only did it to try to make leaving easier for me, and for her, but it didn't help. Lynn was just so excited to be going back to see Michael, who she had been pining for as of late. Edward teased her about this, saying things like, "Are you going to give him a big juicy kiss as soon as you see him?" These comments made me uncomfortable, sounding like the kids teasing at school. Lynn would tell him to grow up or leave her alone, and Mum would echo these sentiments. Edward would chuckle in his devious sneer.

Dinnertime finally came around. Mum had a roast cooking in the oven with potatoes, squash and Yorkshire pudding. It all smelled so good but was making the trailer unbearably hot. We took our plates full of the delicious dinner outside to eat on lawn chairs. The air was cooling slightly as the sun got lower, a train was passing by again and the grain elevator stood out proudly in the fading light.

I wasn't very hungry for my favorite dinner. My tummy felt full of loneliness already. Everyone else talked and laughed as if they didn't know what was happening. I felt that I was dying, alone. Then, that moment came that I did not want, "Well, Tink, I guess this is it, I have to say good-bye," whispered Pat. It was as if my world exploded, the gravity was gone, and all that made it work stopped. I sobbed hysterically. "Come on Tink. You'll see me again. Who knows it might be next summer even." A whole year away? At 9, that was a lifetime! I knew I had to pull myself together. I didn't want him to remember me like this but it was too hard to stop. I started to hiccup trying to stop the onslaught.

"We can write letters all the time and you can tell me all about your friends and school. I'll write and tell you about the boring stuff I do here on the prairie," coached Pat trying to make me happy. Mum brought me some ginger ale to make the hiccups stop. My head felt so heavy, like one of those bobble head dolls, and my tummy felt like a churning volcano. Was this the way my life would be? The hardest moments in my life were always in saying good-bye to Pat. I needed more strength. "Come on, Tink. Give Pat a hug good-bye and we'll color in your book together," offered Corinne for support. At thirteen she could be pretty obnoxious but, at times like this, I couldn't make it without her.

I hugged Pat until I thought my arms were breaking. I did not want to let him go! He meant so much to me! I could not look at him as he pulled away. He hugged each member of the family, telling them all to take care of themselves and telling Mum to take special care of me. I watched the police car drive away. An hour later, as we were getting into the loaded station wagon, I saw it drive by again very slowly.

The long drive home began. It was a difficult decision whether to have the windows down for the wind, or put up with the heat to keep the skunk smell on the outside! The route home was to be the same as on the way there. We were at our first campsite by 7:30. It was light still on the prairie at this time of evening, but quite dark here in the mountains. It was a challenge to set up camp in the dim light with emotionally tired people. Tempers were quick to flare and feelings easily crushed.

We girls all went to the pump to rinse our faces and brush our teeth. On our way back to the camp, we passed Scott and Edward headed to the pump for the same reason. "Good timing. Corinne and I will change before you get back then," said Lynn speaking to Edward. Mum wanted to check how the ice was holding out in the cooler. She went to the car to check it before she changed for bed. I went to the car to change for bed, and Corinne and Lynn got to the tent first. Lynn had just removed all of her day clothes and was about to slip her nightgown over her head, when Edward walked in! "Ahh!" Lynn screamed as she clutched her nightgown trying to hide herself, "Why didn't you ask if we were finished dressing before just barging in?!" Her face flushed with embarrassment, shame, and anger. "Oh, ho, ho," in his devilish chuckle laughed Edward, "I thought you would have been done a long time ago," as if a long time had even passed? "I'm sick of all your little accidents, bumping into woman, saying childish teases, walking in when and where you don't belong! I think you have a serious problem," shouted Lynn. "Oh, listen to Miss High and Mighty herself. Anybody could have walked in here like that, you wouldn't have been upset if it was your lover boy," retorted Edward. "There you go again! Grow up! November can't come soon enough so I can get away from you," she screamed. "What's going on in here? You guys are going to wake the whole campsite," asked Mum coming in from outside. "Oh, you know how these young girls are, always over reacting," Edward answered in his evil chuckle. "Just keep him away from me and I'll be fine," answered Lynn not wanting to cause trouble between her Mum and her husband. Corinne was already snuggled down into her sleeping bag, hoping the problem would blow over.

The next morning the air was filled with tension. We all so wanted to have a perfect family but some of us now realized that there was something wrong in the mix. Hopefully, it would just be a matter of time before the glitch could be smoothed out. With all our hearts, we wanted this! For our Mother's sake, we needed this problem with Edward to be just "girl's over-reacting". It was just a haunted gut feeling. Something you couldn't quite put your finger on but, we three daughters all felt it, although we never spoke about it. That would make it too real. Then we would have to do something about it and none of us could do that to our Mother.

We had our little boxes of cereal for breakfast. Mum and Edward had their tea and a tea bun. I guess we were all anxious to be home because we were packed up, cleaned up and on the road within an hour. The road construction that had held us up for hours on the way to Saskatchewan was finished now, so we just sailed on through. We thought that if we just pushed it a little, maybe we could be on a ferry to the island tonight!

We pulled up to an A&W for some quick hamburgers to eat on the road and a jug of root beer, thereby saving us an hour or so from stopping to eat. It seemed very hot and humid here so our windows were down while we waited for our food. Then we realized why the car-hop had looked so disgusted at our car, it still smelled of skunk! We continued our quest to the coast, stopping only once at a gas station to refuel and so Hanna could use the washroom.

We made it to the ferry for the 9 P.M. sailing! Everyone screwed up their noses as they squeezed passed our car on the crowded deck of the ferry. It was so embarrassing that it still smelled of skunk! What a rush it had been to get here, but we were all so happy to get home that night. Lynn could hardly wait until the next morning to call Michael. It was after 11P.M. when we got home so she had to wait. Edward started to make a smart comment about her having to wait to talk to "lover boy", but a disapproving look from Mum stopped him in his tracks.

Why didn't we tell Pat how uncomfortable the situation was with Edward? Probably because we had no hard evidence that there was anything wrong, just our gut feelings. Pat believed that he had left us with the perfect family, why should we destroy that for him?

Chapter 25

The following morning, Edward went to get Cocoa, from the kennel that he was boarding at. There were some extra charges, on his bill, as Cocoa had chewed all the wood around the metal hinges, getting the door off! We saw the door and were amazed, he had actually chewed through 2" of wood in two spots! He must have had splinters in his gums! We would never send him to a kennel again.

My teddy bear stayed on my bed, ready to cuddle in a moment's notice. The white cowboy hat was another matter. Everyone had said how 'good' it looked on me that it actually made me feel pretty, when I normally felt ugly and awkward, so it felt right to buy the hat. Now it just seemed tacky and would forever sit on my closet shelf. I made my bed and did my chores, then went out into the back yard, wanting to be somewhere else. I sat on the moss-covered rocks overlooking the Inlet dreaming of, and wishing for, magical times. If only I knew that the love of my life was living where I was looking across the water!

School started up again the week after. I was grade 4, Corinne grade 7 for a second try, and Scott grade 11 at the senior high. Lynn was very busy with wedding plans and she picked her best friend, Heather to be her Maid of honor. Heather's father was in charge of the dry docks, so they lived in the most beautiful home. A mansion built in the early 1900's with plenty of oak paneling and the most beautiful, sweeping staircase with banisters of solid. This was all behind the guarded gates of the dry docks. She and Pat had dated once or twice and she dreamed that, when Pat came home from his posting in Humboldt, he would propose marriage to her and she would say yes. Then she and Lynn would be sister-in-laws! Typical girlish imaginings!

Lynn's wedding plans had Scott as an usher, Michael's sister Cindy, and our sister Corinne as bridesmaids, and I as the flower girl. Michael had chosen two of his friends as a best man, and a second usher. I went with my Mum and Eddy (as Edward was called by Lynn and Scott) to his cousin's house. She was going to sew the flower girl dress for me. The fabric was beautiful. Emerald green, satin brocade and Lynn had chosen a pattern of a simple bodice with cap, short sleeves and a flared, knee length skirt. Edward's family were kind enough to refer to me as their niece or cousin but I felt awkward, because I didn't even know them. I really appreciated them including me but I needed more time to get to feel like part of their family.

Lynn, Corinne and I were busy for weeks making both white and pink flowers out of Kleenex to decorate the cars with on the wedding day. We had cut two large hearts, each 2ft tall out, of cardboard. We then covered them with pink flowers, with the words Lynn and Mike done in white flowers in the middle. Since we live in a rainforest, we covered the hearts with plastic from dry cleaner bags and tied one each to the front of the three cars that would be used to transport the attendants of the wedding party. On the wedding day, we would have the ushers decorate the cars.

Then there were the three "showers" to attend. These were all surprise gift parties for Lynn. One shower was given by our Aunt Betty. On the day of this party, Lynn believed that she was going to Aunt Betty's house to pick up some decorative, silver, horse shoes that she would carry under her bouquet, for luck, on her wedding day. Today, she and Michael had spent many hours painting the new house that they were going to rent. Lynn was exhausted and covered with paint, but she knew it would only take a Moment and Aunt Betty would understand her wearing her old worn out jeans all covered in paint! She had no idea that all those people would be there! She was so embarrassed but it gave us something to giggle about, even years later.

Heather gave a shower one evening at her beautiful home. I remember feeling like a princess, walking around in her castle like abode. Another of Lynn's good friends gave the third shower. At each shower, they served those special little sandwiches, tarts and treats! Lynn received many good gifts, including baking pans and trays. She would fill these over the years with her delicious buns, cakes and goodies that she would be well known for.

The wedding day was soon upon us. I, being the flower girl, would be the first to walk down the aisle. I was to step with 1 foot, count one a thousand, two a thousand, before I took another step. And continue that all the way down the aisle. This was to set the tempo for the procession and it was very important! I had been worried about doing this. I even felt sick to my tummy, until I took my third step. Then, I realized I loved all the people smiling at me, and the aisle seemed too short.

This was such a special time for Lynn. She was appreciative to Edward for covering the expenses for flowers, the hall, the dinner, invitations, dresses, etc. She tried to never think again of his invasions into her privacy. Now she was married and in her own home with Michael.

I got more involved in my after-school functions. At nine, I joined Girl Guides after finishing 3 years in Brownies. I focused in on doing what it took to earn badges, and made Christmas crafts for charities. It was a great group of girls and leaders to spend time with, but I told none of them about my discomforts at home.

I was playing pool in the rec room downstairs, when Mum called down to tell me dinner was ready and asked that I tell Edward as well as his hearing was not good enough to hear her from this distance. I put the cue stick back on the rack and walked to the workshop to tell Dad dinner was ready. He wasn't in the workshop, but I heard a noise in the oil tank room. I was startled to see him coming out of that room, looking very red in the face! "I just came to tell you dinner is ready" I said. He looked so guilty as he showed me he had a licorice pipe in his hand. "I guess you caught me. I just went into my stash of goodies. I'll have to save it for desert now" said Edward. We went upstairs for dinner and there was no mention of where he had been or of his "stash".

Corinne and I didn't have to share a bedroom anymore. Corinne moved into the den that used to be Lynn's bedroom. She made her room so cute and cozy. I wished that I had her decorating ability. She was very happy to have a little distance between the two of us. Corinne mistakenly thought I was a little "tattle tell." Last year, when she was in grade six, Mum bought her a new pair of shoes for school. She was told not to wear them until school started next week but, when Mum and Dad were out, and Corinne's friends asked her to meet them at a house a mile away, she went wearing her new shoes. I didn't even know about it. When Mum got home hours later, Corinne was grounded for 2 weeks for wearing her new shoes. When Corinne asked Mum how she knew, Mum said, "A little birdie told me so." Corinne assumed that I was the bird. She didn't realize until years later that Mum was suspicious of her and just looked at the bottom of her shoes to see that they had been worn.

Chapter 26

Looking back over the years to my family at this time, it is very hard for me to write about how it was. We lived in such denial then, all trying to have that wonderful family we dreamed of. All except for Corinne. The only truly strong person, who could face life as it was, without candy coating it. She started speaking up for herself, accusing Edward of sneaking about and going into her room, uninvited, at different times. He kept denying it.

Our parents sent Corinne to a psychiatrist! Our Mother was certain there was probably a traumatic memory that Corinne had from our biological father that made her have these unjust suspicions with Edward. Corinne chose not to tell the psychiatrist her problems, to save face for her Mother, so she wouldn't talk with him. He suggested for her to talk to the wall then, and she wondered who was crazy? She often asked me if I thought she was crazy. Did I believe her about Edward going into her room? Did I ever see him going in or out? I wanted to believe her but I hadn't ever seen or heard anything.

Several months later, Scott came home early one day from school, not feeling well. He was just coming out of the washroom when Corinne's bedroom door opened and Edward walked out. Corinne was just coming up the back stairs from school when she heard Edward stuttering some muffled excuse to Scott about why he was coming out of Corinne's room. "Her closet has the only entrance to the attic and I needed to check on our antennae," Edward explained.

Aghast Corinne stammered, "Is that why you've been going into my room all those times? If that were why, why wouldn't you just have told us, instead of denying it? You were trying to drive me crazy, and make everyone else think I was nuts!" She looked at Scott to see how it was impacting on him. He seemed to have accepted Edward's explanation without hesitation. It had never seemed strange to him that Edward would be going into Corinne's room for any reason.

"Where's Mum? She has to know about this," stated Corinne. "Settle down. It's no big deal," huffed Edward as Mum walked in with a worrisome expression on her face. "Now what," asked Mum apprehensively? "Oh, it's nothing. I was just coming down from doing some antennae work in the attic and Corinne thinks I was doing something to her," he answered in a shaky voice, mimicking how Corinne would have sounded if she were losing her mind. "I didn't sound like that and I would have been fine all along, if you had just told me that you were doing antennae work. But, you didn't tell me that, and THAT'S SUSPICIOUS! Why wouldn't you tell me the truth?" Corinne asked accusingly.

I realized then not to speak to anyone about my problems, or I might be sent to the psychiatrist. No wonder we lived denying the truth even to ourselves.

Our Mum started having nightmares, reliving and acting out her dysfunctional life with our first Dad. She would find herself sleepwalking again, as she had as a child, only now she would awake doing such things as peering out a crack in the door to the darkness outside. She would wake terrified and unable to go back to sleep with fear. She started seeing the same psychiatrist that she had sent Corinne to.

Scott was 16, had his driver's license, and spent most of his free time working to make money. He wanted to save up to buy a boat. Edward had finished building Scott's bedroom in the basement. Scott finally moved into his own room complete with a large built in closet!

A little girl began visiting her grandparents who were our neighbors. She saw me pushing my baby buggy on my driveway one day and asked if she could play with me. It was such fun for me to play with someone younger than myself. She was exactly the same size as my walking doll, so she fit all of her clothes! We played house for hours and she would be my little girl and would change into the appropriate clothes for the situation. She wore pajamas for bed time, party dress for party times, etc. We enjoyed playing together, until Edward came in and said to me, "Don't you think it's a little rude that you keep helping her change?" We had never thought anything wrong with doing that. We were playing house in which I was her Mum, of course I would help her change. The look on Edward's face, and the tone of his voice as he said that to me suddenly made it so disgustingly revolting that I told her it was time to go home and we never played together again.

At school this year, I had two single ladies as teachers. They would both have been 40 or 50 years old, and had travelled around much of the world together. Miss Walker taught us Reading, Arithmetic and Science. Miss Taylor taught Social Studies and P.E. My favorite was learning about Egypt! After school, in my backyard, I would often sit on the rocks by the water and imagine myself to be floating on a barge on the Nile.

Christmas was quiet. Pat did not come home, but Lynn and Michael joined us for Christmas dinner. Michael's Mum was very ill in the hospital with cancer, so they had to leave right after dinner to go and be with her. Michael's father and sister had moved away from our street into the apartments across the inlet from us. Christie Point Apartments. These apartments currently housed the man who would become my husband and I would also one day rent an apartment there with my husband and daughter. At this time however, I had no idea how important those apartments would be to me.

We again received many nice gifts for Christmas. My favorite, was a box of tiny cake mixes with tiny metal cake pans. I had actually asked for the easy bake oven but when my Mum saw that it only baked by a light bulb, she realized the cakes and pans could be baked in a conventional oven just as well. Our stockings were full and Corinne and I were each given a very expensive pair of slacks with a matching sweater. Corinne's was blue and mine was pink. I could imagine our Mother shopping for these outfits. She would have spent hours looking for "just the right thing" but, unfortunately, they were only right to her. Sisters at 9 and 13 do not want matching outfits! Nor would we want polyester pants or heavy knit sweaters. We were disappointed that our Mum seemed to not really know us, to think that these would be even close to what we would like. It always is difficult for busy Mums to stay in touch with their children. Especially in our Mum's case, with everything she had faced in her life. She was such a kind, timid woman that she was easily overwhelmed.

Chapter 27

Pat came home at Easter with quite a surprise! He waited until we were all home together and then he announced, "I've finally met the woman of my dreams. I asked her to marry me, and she said yes. She had been married before and was left a widow after her husband was killed in an industrial accident. She was left to raise her two adorable daughters, one three years old and the other 18 months. They live in a mobile home in a small town in my patrol area." He had just received a new patrol area 6 weeks ago, with a promotion to corporal. He had brought us pictures, so we could see for ourselves what a great deal he was getting.

In the pictures was a tall, slim woman with mid length hair styled just right. She was a secretary for the only lawyer in town and was always well dressed in clothes she had sewn herself. She appeared so poised, and had her hair and make-up just right. Her girls were 3 and 5 years old now and they too were always smartly dressed with their hair in buns or matching pony-tails.

They were to be Pat's new family and I suddenly felt like I lost him forever! My eyes spilled over with silent tears and I hoped they would go unseen but it was not to be. "What's up, Tink? I thought you'd be happy for me," said Pat looking completely dumbfounded. I could not answer for fear of letting the flood gates overwhelm us all, or that the sickness in my tummy would start me vomiting. "She's just afraid you won't love her anymore," explained Corinne. Once again, she knew exactly how I felt and now that it was out in the open the sobs let go. "Oh, come on Tink. You will always be my first girl! I will love you forever!" responded Pat giving me a big hug. "The wedding will be in June of next year and I hope you will be able to come and meet your new family." Of course, it would be up to Edward if we were to make the long drive again. He and Mum would have to talk about it for a while.

A few weeks after Easter, Mum and Dad were very serious one morning. Mum said to Corinne and I, "Dad will drive you both to school today, there has been a terrible accident."

"Is Scott all right," asked Corinne as her eyes clouded up with tears. She was always preparing for the worst. "Oh, yes. It wasn't one of us. A teen-aged girl was murdered near here," explained our Mother and she continued, "Dad will drive you to school and back for the next few days until they find out who's responsible."

We felt very scared but were thankful for the ride to school. We could even leave a half hour later so I would be able to watch morning cartoons! The kids at school were all very excitable. There had never been a murder here before, that we were aware of. Teacher's walking the grounds were trying to settle everyone down. "This is not a reason for excitement, people! Remember a young woman has lost her life and her family is very remorseful. You need to have respect and sympathy," Mr. Burchill said. Everyone grew quiet. The bell rang a moment later and the chattering began again, even more animated than before.

Miss Alicems began, "Class, I realize there has been a traumatic event that has gotten your attention this morning. Now it is time for class and I do expect you to concentrate on the subject at hand, Mathematics!" School went on as usual for the next few weeks, other than Corinne and I getting rides to and from.

By the third week the police had made an arrest. Miss Alicems explained, "Class you will hear that the man arrested and charged with murder is a brother to Douglas Smith. A gasp of shock filled the air as we all turned to look at our classmate's empty chair. Yes, he is not here today. I am sure his family is in complete turmoil dealing with this situation. What I expect from you is that when Douglas does return to class, that you will treat him as you always have. His brother has not been proven guilty of this deed, only charged with it. No matter the outcome of his trial, Douglas is the same nice, shy, little boy he was before this happened. He has not changed. This will be a real test to see how understanding and mature you people can be." She was right. It was a real test of our character and, in my judgment, we didn't fare too well. Some of the boys did tease

Douglas about it and he did withdraw further. I felt very sad for him but did not know how to make it better.

The night of the arrest, it was all over the papers. Edward was reading it aloud to Mum as she was cooking dinner. I heard him read the victim had her hands tied behind her back and then was raped and choked to death. Douglas's brother, Lester Smith, had worked part-time as a janitor at our elementary school. He lived at home with his parents and siblings and he suffered from a diminished mental capacity.

"Here you've been driving the girls back and forth to school, and he worked right there with them all the time," gasped Mum. "They shouldn't let those people near our children." "Well, especially a young man his age. He would see all those girls and get ideas," suggested Edward. "I mean men have needs whether they are handicapped or not."

"Did he strangle her around her neck," I asked Mum as I entered the room. "Oh, you shouldn't have been listening," sighed Mum, "What makes you think she was strangled to death." "Dad read that she choked to death." I explained. I still felt awkward calling Edward, Dad. I was thankful to him for all he did for me but there was still something that made me not want to be close to him, something that made me hate myself for not letting us have the perfect family!

"Well it says that she choked to death," offered Edward, "But you know what it's like in our forests, there would be a lot of fir needles and broken up oak leaves on the path where they found her laying on her stomach. She probably kept screaming and sucked that debris down her throat. If she wouldn't have screamed, she could still be alive now. Smith probably shouldn't be charged with murder if she didn't die from his hand." "I don't want to talk about this anymore," pleaded Mum, holding her hands up to stop, "this is all too morbid."

We did not talk about it anymore but it didn't stop us thinking about it. I was sad for Douglas. He had always been shy and quiet, but now he seemed to disappear entirely. Edward read every article that was ever printed about the murder in the paper, but he never read them aloud anymore. He also kept the articles in a drawer in his room.

Chapter 28

Grade 4 was coming to a close. I continued to spend many weekends away, either at Lynn and Michael's house, at my girlfriends or at Guide camps.

The next few weeks of school were filled with government exams; designed to keep the teachers marking equally for passing grades. These were the forms that contained a question with 5 possible answer boxes and, with an HB pencil, you filled in only one box. I always imagined someone marking these tests with a blank answer form of circles cut in the right spots to reveal the correct answer below. It would show up blackened, through the cut circle if the answer was correct. I dreamed they would not align the answer sheet correctly over my test paper and, I feared, they would mark all of mine wrong!

The school year ended the next month, with the traditional track meet being held on a perfect summer day in the final week. At dinner that night, Mum and dad told us we were going to Pat's wedding next June. We would start buying things now while they were on sale, to be ready well in advance of travel next year. The following day, Mum took me shopping for summer shorts and tops. We found some really cute sets. The tops were called "pop tops". They had an elasticized edge just above the tummy. We bought these to fit me for what was left of this summer but, large enough, to wear on our trip to the wedding.

Summer was always most difficult for me. School stopped and all of our extracurricular activities ended. I spent day after day playing with Donna, either on our bikes, with Barbies or building a fort in the lot. I even went to church with her family on Sundays.

One day, when she wasn't home, I rode my bike to the park at the corner of our road. My bike was leaning against the metal standard that supported the swings and I was drifting on a swing, daydreaming, when I heard someone say, "Hi Hanna. Do you live around here?" I was shocked back into the current time and space, and was amazed to see a boy who was in my class, Wesley Foster. "Yes, I live just down this road," I answered thinking how I had never spoken to him before.

He hung around the park with me all that afternoon. He showed me all the tricks he could do on the crossbar between the two, metal, upside down V shaped legs supporting the swings. We talked about the year we had with our grade 4 classes and wondered who our teachers would be for grade 5.

"I hope we will be in the same class," said Wesley and, "Will you come here to play tomorrow?" I suddenly felt a little embarrassed; realizing that it was almost getting dark and I hadn't even noticed the time had gone by! "I'm going to be late for dinner and I'll get in trouble from my Mum," I muttered. "Will you come here tomorrow, about three?" Wesley repeated shouting at me as I was starting to ride home. "Oh, probably," I answered not really thinking that I had just been asked to meet up with a boy. "I'll be here waiting. Don't forget," he yelled to me. I heard him over the distance I had already ridden away from the park.

Mum was quite angry when I got home and everyone was already half-finished eating. "Where were you? I was getting worried," atoned Mum firmly to show her disapproval.

"I was just at the park and didn't realize how late it was," I offered in apology. "Was Donna with you," she asked? It was uncomfortable for me to answer this. "No, she was out with her family. I was just playing alone." I really was playing alone. Wesley had just joined me and I didn't want to add that, or I would be teased by Scott and Corinne. "Try to be on time or we'll have to come looking for you next time," added Mum so I would be more careful in the future.

The next morning, I did some chores and then played with my Barbie's for a while. After lunch, the "ice cream lady's van" came around with its nursery tunes blaring. Mum gave me a quarter to get a Revello. As I paid the lady my quarter, she said, "Just think, this time next week you will be back in school!" I didn't quite understand what she meant so she added, "It's almost three o'clock and school starts next week. At three o'clock next week, you will still be in school"

I walked away in silence as I thought to myself that Wesley would be at the park now waiting for me! I didn't want to hurt his feelings but I really didn't want to be his girlfriend either. I sat on the lawn eating my ice cream trying to decide. By the time I was done, I had decided. Wesley will probably have left by now, I was so late, but I would ride down on my bike just to see.

As I got closer, I could see there was no one at the park. I felt a little disappointed that Wesley wasn't still waiting. Sad that I would have hurt his feelings but somehow at ease that I wouldn't have to be anyone's girlfriend. A voice came from the other side of the tennis court. "Well, you decided to come after all? Did you have trouble getting away from your Mum?" Looking more carefully, I could see Wesley sitting on the curb around the court. "Oh hi, no I was just busy," I answered, feeling as if I had been caught doing something very embarrassing. "I'll have you a race to see who can pump the highest on the swings."

We enjoyed a carefree hour on the swings, talking about school and friends. Then he said, "I have something for you." I watched as he pulled something, that looked like a 3" ball of paper, out of his pocket. "Why? It isn't my birthday or anything," I uttered out of complete confusion. "It just smells so pretty that it reminds me of you, and I want you to have it," he said eying his shoes as he passed me the wad of paper. As I looked at the paper to take a hold of it, he kissed my cheek and then ran to his bike saying, "I gotta go. My Mum will be looking for me." Feeling bewildered by this unexpected gift, I wondered if I had just had my first kiss? Well, except for that one from Darren.

A very heavy glass bottle fell out of the paper. It was actually a very pretty, glass or crystal, atomizer. It looked like columns of glass that were twisted in a spiral, with a gold pump to squeeze to release a mist of perfume. I did not wear perfume yet and didn't really like the smell of it but was astonished that Wesley had given it to me. By the time I was aware enough to say "Thank-you." Wesley was long gone. I rewrapped my bottle in the paper and set it in the blue plastic basket on my handlebars. Then I rode for home.

I told my family about my gift at the park. Every detail except for the kiss. "Well, Tink, we had better start watching out, you're growing up! Soon it will be an engagement party," teased Scott. "I hope he won't get into trouble for having given you what looks like his Mum's perfume," offered Mum. Now I was worried that Wesley might be in trouble. I wondered if I should give it back? The next time I was at the park, he was not there. Nor did I see him again until school started in the fall. Then he paid no attention to me and I thought that it was just as well.

Chapter 29

The following morning, Mum woke me saying that Dad was going to take her to the hairdresser. Corinne and I would be home alone for about two hours. I got up and joined Corinne at the kitchen table, where she was having breakfast. Mum had given us the list of the few jobs we were to do while she was gone. Dad would be back in two hours to check that we were still okay. Mum and Dad left right away, so Mum wouldn't miss her appointment time. Corinne quickly finished breakfast and raced to do the chores she had been given. I left the table and went to make my bed. As soon as that was done, I began dusting the living room, dining room, my Mum's room and my room.

Corinne came in and said, "I have finished my chores, including all the dishes we had to do. I'm going to go to Brenda's now to finish our homework project. You will be okay for 20 minutes alone, won't you?" I replied, "Sure, for 20 minutes I won't be afraid alone. Please don't be longer." "I shouldn't be any longer than that, but you know where Brenda's house is, I won't be far away" Corinne added. With that she left the house.

After finishing the last of my jobs, I went downstairs to play pool. After playing about 10 minutes, I started to feel hungry (especially when I thought of Dad's "stash of goodies" in the oil tank room). I laid the pool cue on the table and headed to that room. The smell from the oil tank was very strong but at least the room was well lit by the light from the window. I turned to my left and saw a shelf covered with magazines and the box of licorice pipes. I helped myself to one of the licorice and then I noticed that the pictures in the magazines were of naked women! They were all very beautiful, some partially dressed, just their breasts were bare. Some were even holding their breasts as if they were showing them off.

Then I heard a car pulling into our carport. I suddenly felt sick! Dad was home and Corinne wasn't! She would be in trouble for having left me at home alone. I decided to stay hidden. Perhaps he would think Corinne had taken me with her. I hoped Dad wouldn't stay too long. I froze when I heard him come in the door. He started working at his bench, like he was packing up things to take to the car, and I thought maybe my plan would work and he wouldn't know that I was there! Then to my horror I heard his footsteps coming my way.

"Hanna, what are you doing in there?" questioned Edward. Looking up from where I was crouched, I saw him staring down at me. "I'm sorry I came to get a licorice pipe". "You should be sorry! That's stealing!" The look on his face filled me with terror. I knew something bad would happen. Then I noticed a huge wolf spider in the room a few feet from me. Once again, I focused on anything but Edward. I put my fear in to the spider, instead of Edward. That's when Hanna left the room and a second alter ego was produced, Erin. She would remember Edward stepping in to the oil room saying, "You dirty, little girl! You were reading these magazines, weren't you? Did you get excited by looking at the pictures? Are your boobs growing as big as those women's?" With this he lifted my "pop top", to see that my chest was growing into little boobs with puffy nipples. "Oh yeah, look at this" he remarked Touching them with his finger to see if they would contract. "Wow, will your babies be happy!" He exclaimed, with a flushed look of excitement on his face. "They can latch on to those no problem." His face frowned and then he added "I guess I had better get packed up with Mr. Brown's TV to deliver it before I pick up your Mum." Then he loaded them into the car and, to my relief, he drove away. From that day forward, I was terrified of spiders. Years later, I even began vomiting when a nephew tossed a plastic one at me and it accidentally got tangled in my hair.

Chapter 30

The next day was Donna Billingsley's birthday. My birthday was only two days later, so her Mother invited Carol and I to sleep over at their house. We could celebrate our tenth birthdays together. At first, we were having so much fun but then it seemed like one of us would always feel left out. Silly little things would start up arguments, like where our Barbie dolls would go on their dates that night. I would rather bow out of the discussions and let the other girls make the decision, instead of fighting over something so trivial. It was then I decided that three females are a bad mix. Two are great and so are four or more but three is asking for trouble.

A week later, Donna and I signed up with a dance school to start in September. We would learn tap, ballet and folk dances. I would love this and spent the next 7 years being dedicated to the art. Our dance troupe was in many shows, even twice performing at "The Playhouse" downtown! The excitement of learning routines, wearing costumes, dancing on stage and getting my picture in the newspaper, helped me to ignore the realities of home.

September also brought us back to the school. We nervously waited in the court yard, to find our who our teachers would be. We played hop scotch, basketball, jump rope, anything we could to pass the time.

The principal, Mr. Christenson entered the courtyard from the school. He announced that each of the teachers would come out and call all of the students for their classes. They began with the grade 1's. It took about a while to call all of the little guys. Then the grade 2 teacher called all of her students, and so on for grade 3 and 4. Finally, it was time for the grade 5 class. Mrs. Gray stepped forward. She announced that there were so many grade fives, we had enough to form 2 classes. She began listing off the children for her class. Donna Billingsley was one of them, but I was not. Then it was Mr. Richard's turn to call the students for his class. I was called for this class. There were many kids I knew, but none that I really considered friends of mine. Mr. Richard instructed us to follow him into our new classroom.

"I will ask you all to remain standing. The tallest people I would like seated at the back of the class. I will point out which ones you are. I only know a few of your names yet. Stephen Arnold, Jeffrey Banks, and you, young man in the brown jacket, and this young lady." he said pointing to me will fill the last seats in the rows. Everyone else can take any other seat for now. Mr. Richard was the first male teacher I had ever had. It felt strange to me but he was a very nice man.

That fall, Corinne, now 14, signed up with an all-female drum corp. They were very good. Each girl carried a snare drum on a strap over her shoulders. They wore white pleated skirts and white shirts with a small red vest over top. On their heads, they wore a white fur cap. Marching in many parades, they travelled to various cities across the country. She developed a real camaraderie with many of the girls and would escape from home to their places for weekends. She became especially close with Gloria, who was an only child and was very close with her Mother. Corinne confided in them about how it was for her at home. She would stay more and more weekends with Gloria. She even began to call home on Sunday night to see if she could stay to finish an assignment for class and then go to school with Gloria in the morning. Mum did not like this situation but gave in on occasions to keep the peace.

June of grade 5 was so exciting. I did well on the final exams and was promoted to grade six. The day after school finished, we packed our tent trailer in preparation for our trip to Saskatchewan for Pat's wedding. The trailer had been parked on the grass beside our carport. Edward opened it up, to let the fresh air in. It smelled quite musty from being closed up in the damp, West Coast air for a full year.

Mum gave Corinne and I, the sheets and blankets to make up the bed for Edward and her. She also gave us three sleeping bags, one for each Corinne, Scott, and I. We laid one sleeping bag on each of 2 cot bunk beds (Scott would be sleeping in the car again). Then we placed these cots one beside each other on Mum and Dad's bed. The pole legs for our cot beds were kept in the cupboard beneath Mum and Dad's bed. We also packed a first aid kit, eight toilet paper rolls, two pots stacked together, a frying pan and that all-important kettle for Mum's tea. She put five Melmac dinner plates, three plastic glasses, two mugs and some cutlery into a box. This box could be taken out as needed and put on the picnic table.

Then we chose our clothes to wear during the trip. I was excited to wear the dress that Corinne had worn to Mum and Dad's wedding. I had grown so much taller than Corinne was when she wore the dress, that it was now a mini-skirt on me, which was in style. She got a new skirt and blouse for Pat and Eileen's wedding. Scott got a new pair of dress slacks, with a new shirt and tie to match, as the weather would be far too warm to wear a jacket.

Once packed, Edward closed up the trailer and hooked it up to the car. He wanted us ready to go in the morning, to catch the 7:00 am ferry to the mainland. This meant that we had to be up at 5:00 am, dressed, faces washed and ready to leave. I was to be in bed by 9pm, with visions of all the things I might have forgotten to pack running through my head. 5am came much too soon! We were in the car, pulling out of the drive way by 6. This trip, Corinne, Scott and I were sitting on the back seat. Lynn would be riding in her own car, with Michael. They were to leave a few days after us because they could only get a week off work. They had to pack a tent to stay overnight on route. This was very exciting for the newlyweds.

The trip passed without incident and the wedding was beautiful. I was still jealous of Pat's new daughters place in his life but was happy to see my brother so happy and to be gaining more family members.

# Chapter 31

When we returned home, Edward installed a remote controller onto the TV antennae. This allowed him to reposition the antennae by turning the remote in the basement. Still Corinne would find him slipping in and out of her room. He always had an excuse prepared such as the remote being jammed or something.

At 17, Scott had bought himself a small, older cabin cruiser with an inboard motor. He was extremely proud of his boat and would always ask me to go along for the ride. I remember one day especially! It had rained quite heavily that night and there was a good 5-6" of water in the boat. This was not a problem for Scott, as he was quite a wizard with mechanics, and had hooked up a pump to get rid of the water.

We started off from our dock and headed out into the Inlet. It was a very nice, sunny day and I was holding the tiller to keep the boat going in a small circle while Scott set up his pump. He started it up and it worked quite smoothly, spewing water over the side of the boat while Scott held the hose. However, it was rather noisy!

I was looking to the starboard side of the boat when suddenly, what seemed like a wall of water, was in my face! I started trying to blow the water away from my mouth and thrashing my arms about. I was sure I must have hit something and we were sinking! Thankfully the water stopped smothering me and I heard Scott laughing! I blinked the last of the water from my eyes to see Scott standing in the boat, doubled up with laughter!

"I'm sorry Tink, it was my fault!" Scott tried to explain while laughing hysterically. "I reached for a wrench, to adjust the noise on the pump, and had to let go of the drainage hose for just a second. The pressure was so much that it shot the hose straight up and into your face! It took me just a minute to see what was happening and another to get it under control.

Are you alright? Here's a towel, dry off and I'll take you home." It was a day that brought laughter to us for years to come and was just one of many trips on one of Scott's boats that will always be remembered!

That September of 1966, I was eleven and entering grade 6. Corinne was 15 and in grade 9 at the junior high. This was the same school that Pat, Lynn and Scott had all been through. She did very well in sewing class and was always interested in fashion. By sewing some of her own clothes, she learned how to have a better wardrobe for less money. She made two really cute outfits, patterned blouses that would go under overall styled dresses. They were basic A-lined tunic dresses with the shoulders cut off and overall straps to hold the front to bodice height. One was yellow and the other blue. I loved them and she let me borrow them. Their light cotton fabric was so cool in the warm, spring-like fall weather we were experiencing.

Scott graduated from High School at 18. He had a steady girlfriend at this time, Lori. She went to the same school as Corinne and was in some of her classes. Corinne often came home with rumors she had heard about Lori. We tried to ignore the gossip when our brother started talking of marriage.

That summer, Scott worked full-time with a painting company that Edward worked for. Scott was considered for foreman but needed to take a one-year course in Vancouver. He signed up for the fall course. Lori was very sad that he would be away so much but agreed that it would be good for their future.

Things were still very uncomfortable for Corinne with Edward. One Saturday morning, she came into my room whispering, "Come here I've got to show you something." I followed her into the bathroom where she shut the door behind us. She opened the cupboard that contained the bowl we girls put our soiled panties in for pre-soaking. All of our dirty laundry went into the large wicker basket in the kitchen by the washer, except for our panties. I wondered what she was showing me? This felt a little strange and I began to think that maybe she was losing it!

"You see there are 4 pairs of panties in the bowl," she said, as she carefully separated them so I could see and so they were neatly arranged. "Now wait and see what they look like after Edward has been in here. Hurry let's get back in our rooms, I can hear him coming up the stairs from the basement."

I did exactly what she told me even though my stomach felt queasy! I wanted to ask Mum for her advice but she was at the hairdresser's. I made my bed and got dressed while Dad was in the bathroom. He was taking a long time but he usually did. Finally, I heard the toilet flush and the water run for him to wash his hands. Then the door opened and I heard him walk down the hall and down the basement stairs. I was opening my door just as Corinne opened hers. We both stepped into the bathroom and shut the door behind us. Corinne opened the cupboard and there in the bowl was a tangled mess of panties! I just stood dumbfounded! I couldn't make any sense of this.

"You see. He does this all the time. Oh, my God! There are only 3 pairs left! He has taken my pink ones with him! I will never wear them again!" Corinne gasped in horror. "What is he doing with them? Oh, I have to go out! It makes me sick to think about it!"

I felt a little like I was in a Nancy Drew mystery novel. It was as if I was stuck between two pages, having not fully understood what had happened on the previous page. I had no idea what to expect once the pages turned and now Corinne was leaving. She said, "Tell Mum that I went to Betty's to finish a report for school. Don't worry about what just happened. It's nothing new, it's just you didn't know about it before." That was true but, now that I did know about it, what was I supposed to do with it?

I went for a long bike ride, thinking for hours. It was Saturday and I had ridden into the next school district and was getting a drink from the outdoor water fountain at their elementary school. I was tired from riding and didn't know just where I wanted to go from here. I leaned my bike against an outcrop of granite rocks and climbed to the top of them to sit and think. It was another beautiful, sunny day. This confused me even more since my life felt cloudy and unclear. Sitting on my rock perch above the school playground, I noticed some younger kids watching me while they were playing. Soon their curiosity brought them over to ask me some questions.

"You look new around here, did you just move in?" One of the little girls asked.

I really didn't want to be asked any questions about myself, or my life, at this point but I didn't want to hurt their feelings so I just said, "No, I'm just passing through." "Did you run away from home?" another little girl asked. Now was my chance to escape from my real world, to be whom-ever I wanted. I began my tale, "Yes, I did leave my home and I'm travelling around with some friends. They are working right now but I have the day off so I'm just riding around to see what there is here. I really should be going though as they will be done work soon."

"Will you be back tomorrow?" asked a little blond with pigtails and saucer blue eyes.

"No, I don't think I'll be by here again because there are so many other places to see" I said as I rode away, waving. I felt somewhat guilty because I had lied but, on the other hand, I sort of felt mysterious and awesome. It taught me a lot, though. No matter what I did the truth was still there. I still had to go home and live my own lie, trying to pretend I was happy.

I arrived to find Mum home with her hair set perfectly, cooking our dinner. Edward was downstairs fixing a television or was he doing something with Corinne's undies? Corinne was staying the night at Betty's. I washed my hands to set the dinner table for four. I really missed Corinne when she wasn't home but the house was calmer.

After dinner, I went down to Donna's house so we could plan our Halloween costumes. We decided that this would probably be our last year to go trick or treating and we would go together. We would wear our alien costumes from dance. They were just our black leotard dance suits, with a florescent pink, satin bib held at the waist by a 3" wide silver, metal-looking belt. On our heads, we wore similar hats. They were made from bleach bottles with one side and the bottom cut away so that they fit on our heads like a hat. They were spray painted to look alien. Donna's was sprayed gold with florescent pink dots stuck all over it and a round plastic ball glued to the top of the bleach bottle opening. Mine was sprayed silver with a 3" TV tube in the hole and two rabbit ears from a T.V standing up on either side of the tube! For Halloween, we added little cover-up jackets made from thick clear plastic bags. We added a florescent pink, satin ruffle trim along the bottom. These were in case of rain. The outfits were really quite impressive and we got a lot of compliments and whistles! I always felt so ugly and thought people only whistled to be kind!

Chapter 32

That Christmas, we were expecting Pat and his family to come home! We were all excited! Corinne, Mum and I each took turns baking different holiday treats. The steamed carrot pudding, mincemeat tarts, brown-eyed Susan cookies, sugar cookies cut into Christmas shapes, ginger bread men and short bread cookies were all family traditions.

We rented two extra cots to put in my room for Jennifer and Valerie. Corinne would sleep in her old bed so that Pat and Eileen could have her double bed and her room. Lynn, Michael, Grandma and Corrina would join us for Christmas dinner. We figured if we put the two extra leaves in the dining room table and brought the kitchen table in on the end, we could comfortably seat everyone.

Now it was time to put up and decorate our live fir tree. It was Scott's job to get the tree securely in the stand and to put the colored lights on. Then Corinne and I hung the garland, balls and icicles one strand at a time, to give the tree a lacy, delicate appearance. It was so beautiful but took hours to accomplish! I felt so complete doing things with my siblings.

Finally, Pat's family was due to arrive! Corinne and I were so excited that we had all of our chores done right after breakfast. We sat down to play cards to pass the time. Every time a car went up our street, one of us would run to the window to see if it was them. This time it was Corinne's turn, "It's them!" she screamed. I quickly stacked the cards, put them in the drawer and ran to the door all in one motion.

Corinne had left the door open behind her and was hugging Pat as he was just climbing out of the car. I too was piling on top of Pat, laughing as Pat chuckled, "Come on ladies give a guy some air!" It was then we noticed Eileen on the other side of the car, helping her two little girls out of the back seat, if you could call it that. It had been changed into a whole bed! Pat had put a wooden board from the back of the front seat to the back of the back seat, covered it with a foam mattress and blankets so the girls had a larger area to play Barbies, color, sleep, or whatever passed the driving time.

"You remember my family?" he boasted, beaming with pride. "My wife, your Auntie Eileen and my daughters Jennifer and Valerie?" I never realized, until just typing this now, that even though I called her "Auntie Eileen" all of those years, she was actually my sister-in-law. I always knew that I was Jennifer and Valerie's Aunt, for I would brag to my friends that I was only 11 and an Aunt already!

Mum was at the front door calling, "Please come in and let me see my new Daughter-in-law and Granddaughters!" I watched Pat and his new family walk up the front steps to where Mum was waiting, with outstretched arms, to envelope them in a welcoming embrace. I was so envious. It was not jealousy, as I understand it. I believe to be jealous you would do any back-stabbing thing to get what you want. Instead, I felt I would just pine for their life styles, as Cocoa had pined for Pat when he went away.

Eileen was pretty, very dignified and friendly. She was dressed in light colored coullats (these were all the rage at that time) and matching jacket, with a cool and colorful tank top underneath, perfect for travelling. The outfit was dressy enough, without looking stuffy or uncomfortable. Her sandy blonde hair was cut in a short, trendy style. The girls had on matching cotton short and top sets, Jennifer's in green and Valerie's in pink. Their blonde hair was done in matching, flat buns on the top of their heads. They were both adorable, the perfect family that Pat deserved so much!

Jennifer, the eldest was 7 and very outgoing. She was quite talkative and very athletic doing somersaults and cartwheels on the lawn. The younger one, 5-year-old Valerie, was very shy. She stayed back, holding her Mum's hand as long as she could.

Pat proudly marched up the stairs to Mum's waiting arms. "Well, hello there, Mum," he said, sounding a little embarrassed or humble, "You remember my eldest daughter Jennifer from the wedding? She's pretty smart and outgoing for seven. And my gorgeous wife, Eileen, who will be embarrassed that I said that. Last, but not least, little Valerie. She's 5 now and kind of shy but she'll get used to you."

"Welcome to our home and to our family," Mum crooned as she hugged each one of her new family members. Maybe Corinne and Hanna would take Jennifer and Valerie to play on the swings in the backyard while we adults have a cup of tea." "Sure," announced Corinne as she held out each of her hands, one to Jennifer who grabbed it right away and one to Valerie. "No, I don't wanna go," stammered Valerie clutching her Mother's hand tighter. "Oh, it's okay Valerie, I'll hold your hand until you feel safer," reassured Jennifer. "No, I wanna stay with Mum," demanded Valerie. "Now come on, Val, we talked about this remember?" cajoled Pat. "You can go with Jennifer. Mum and I will just be in the kitchen."

With that said, Valerie took Jennifer's hand and the four of us went to the swing set. Jennifer sat on one side of the teeter-totter style bench, I sat on the other and Corinne started pushing Valerie on one of the swings. Corinne started asking them questions about their school grades, hobbies, friends and other interests. Jennifer was very forthcoming and informative, but Valerie was very shy and aloof. About an hour passed when Valerie spoke, "Jennie? Can we go see Mum now?" "Well, I guess we could go and see if we can come in now?"

The four of us climbed the stairs to the kitchen door, opening it to the smell of roasting chicken. Our parents were not in the kitchen but sitting at the dining room table having tea and cookies. "Well, here's our little ladies now," sighed Pat with pride in his eyes. "Did you guys get to know each other a bit better?" "A little bit. Can we go show them where they will be sleeping while they are here?" asked Corinne. "Sure, you can, and then we'll move to the living room and we can talk about all the things we'll do while we're here," informed Pat.

We four girls went to my bedroom where my twin beds had been joined by two rental beds, making a very cozy bedroom with just enough space to walk between the beds! My dresser had nine drawers of which I had emptied 3, 1 for each of them to use. Then we showed them the bathroom and the drawer for them and their parents to put their toiletries in.

"Wow, two more girls to share the bathroom with," huffed Scott who had just gotten home from work. He was on a 2 week Christmas break from his painting course in, and he always teased us about taking too long when doing our hair, having showers, etc. "I guess you ladies don't curl your hair yet though?" "No, Mummy does that for us!" giggled Jennifer and Valerie.

The five of us went to the living room to join Eileen and Pat. Mum was in the kitchen preparing dinner and was to call Eileen when she could help do something. Edward had gone to his workshop as he had three customer's TV's to repair.

"Well, here's my little brother, if I can still call you that?" Pat said, giving Scott a hand shake and an appraising eye. "I think you've done a fine job growing up and you have quite a career plan, I hear?" "Yeah, I'm just home now for Christmas break, then I'll be back to school for 6 more months of my painting course." Scott spoke with confidence in knowing that his future was secure. "While the bathroom's clear I'll go get a shower. I'll talk to you more, later."

"Well ladies, tomorrow I think we should go to the Enchanted Forest, what do you think?" asked Pat. Jennifer, Valerie and I all looked at each other. None of us knew what it was but it sounded like fun to me! It was agreed that, tomorrow after lunch, we would go there.

Eileen slipped into the kitchen to give Mum a hand with dinner. Corinne and I were called to set the table. This left Pat sitting and talking with his girls. A scene I always envied, remembering how good and safe I had felt sitting talking with my big brother when I was their ages.

Dinner was so much fun again with 11 of us home. Lynn and Michael had also joined us to see Pat and his family. Our dining table only sat eight, so a separate card table was set at the end for Jennifer, Valerie and I. We had a great dinner of roast chicken, mashed potatoes, gravy, peas and carrots, stuffing, cranberry jelly. The adults also had squash. We even had dessert of peach cobbler and ice cream! After dinner, Corinne and I cleared the table and started loading the dishwasher while Mum put the food away and Eileen ran a bath for her two girls. When we finished the dishes, Eileen was read a story to her girls while Corinne and I took turns having baths. It was fun for the four of us to sleep together in the same room, like a pajama party. We were so excited to be going to the "Enchanted Forest" tomorrow, even though we didn't know what it was!

Chapter 33

The next morning, I awoke to Jennifer telling Valerie to be quiet and not wake Corinne or I. I was glad to be awake though. There was much to be excited about and I didn't want to sleep and miss anything! It was just 3 days before Christmas, Pat and Scott were both home and some of us were going to the Enchanted Forest today. Mum was already in the kitchen preparing pancakes, bacon, sausage and eggs for breakfast. As I walked by Corinne's bedroom door, it opened and Eileen said, "Good morning Kerr." Pat had introduced me to Eileen as "Kerr" and her to me as "Auntie Eileen", neither of which were correct but they stuck.

We enjoyed breakfast together and decided that Pat, Eileen, Jennifer, Valerie, Corinne and I would go to the Enchanted Forest together. Scott and Dad had a painting job to do and Mum wanted to get some housework done. We four girls went to make our beds and clean our room. Jennifer, Valerie and I started playing Barbie dolls and Corinne went to talk to her friends on the phone. Scott and Dad went to work and Mum, Pat and Eileen were finishing their tea and talking.

"The four of you make a beautiful family," Mum was saying, "but wouldn't you want to have another child, maybe a boy, a child of "your own"?" With this said, Pat's fist slammed down on the table, causing the tea cups to bounce into the air, "I have two children of "my own" and this is the end of this conversation!" The raised voice brought Jennifer, Valerie and I running to see what it was all about. "Okay ladies. It's all right, I just got a little excited but I'm okay now. We should get ready to go to the Enchanted Forest," explained Pat.

Within the hour, the six of us were in the car on our way. We took a leisurely drive there to show Eileen and the girls a little bit of our city. We drove past the parliament buildings and the harbor, as well as where we used to live when we were growing up. This brought us to the Enchanted Forest at about 2 o'clock. The trees here were so huge and the brush so dense that you couldn't see anything beyond where you were standing. It gave an air of excitement and mysticism! Pat paid the money to enter. The ticket booth looked like a huge pumpkin that was carved out so the lady could stand inside it.

"Okay ladies I have a map that leads us to the first stop. Goldilocks' house with the three bears," Pat told us which paths to take until we reached the cute stone house. It contained a table set with three bowls of porridge. One huge bowl that was still steaming, a medium sized bowl that was almost frosty on the outside from being so cold, and a tiny bowl that was scooped clean and laying on its side, empty. There was also a living room area with three armchairs. A huge one built of stone that would be so hard, a medium sized chair that had fluffy cushions on it. It looked like you would sink into them when you sat and could even smother in them it was so soft. Lastly, a tiny chair that was broken all to pieces! In the bedroom, there were three beds. One huge stone bed, another medium sized bed of feathers and a tiny bed with a little blonde girl, wrapped in a red cloak, sleeping in it!

Pat's map led on to a straw house. Inside there was a little pig dancing by the fire, but outside you could see that the wolf was coming through the forest with his mouth ready to blow the house down. The map led on to the next house built of sticks. Inside we could see a little pig sitting at his table eating dinner but outside you knew the wolf was coming, his big mouth filled with the wind to blow the house down. The next house, as we expected, was brick. In the front yard were the three pigs dancing. Leaning against a tree was a very skinny wolf. He was holding his stomach and his tongue was hanging out. Inside the house, on the walls, were pictures of the houses that the wolf had blown down.

When we left the brick house, we could see a tall castle in the distance. We started running in anticipation of what we might see! When we got closer, the bushes changed to huge thorn bushes. The path we were on was the only way through them. The thorn bushes grew to the height of the castle. Next to the path was a castle window we could look into to see a beautiful canopied bed. The bed was all trimmed in gold with a fluffy, high mattress covered in a lacy pink blanket. Lying on top of the bed was a beautiful, young woman with long black hair. She was sound asleep and we could even see her chest rising as she breathed! The door to her room was opening and, standing waiting to come in, was the prince who had cut the thorns away to get to the castle. According to the story of "Sleeping Beauty" he would kiss the lady, breaking the spell that kept her sleeping, and the thorns around the castle would disappear! We stood looking on longingly at the sweet couple. Then we continued on the path, following the map to the last exhibit.

The last house was just an average wooden house with a magnificent golden carriage beside it. Looking inside the house, we could see four women. One very miserable looking, fat lady in a long dress was pointing her finger at a smaller, pretty, young lady, in a ragged skirt and blouse, who was sweeping the floor with a corn broom. Two, not so pretty, young women, dressed in nice clothes were sitting at the table with hand mirrors, brushes, and lipsticks. It was obviously Cinderella, her Stepsisters and Stepmother. In the carriage sat Cinderella in a beautiful, golden, chiffon evening gown. The bodice was cut low with a sweetheart neckline, puffed, short sleeves, and a full bell-shaped skirt. On her feet was only one crystal slipper. Her hair was so pretty, done up in ringlets with a small diamond tiara. We girls stood in awe gazing at our dream come true.

"Well, ladies, I guess we had better get back to the house as it's nearly dinner time."

We agreed to go but wondered why the "Enchanted Forest" people hadn't finished the story of Cinderella with the Prince coming to get her. Then, just a few steps down the path, we came to a speeding horse with the prince on his back holding a pillow with the glass slipper resting on top of it! We could then dream of the happy ending for Cinderella and the prince but we could not dream of the sad ending to the Enchanted Forest. Years later it was smashed to bits repeatedly by vandals. Some of the realities of life are too hard to bare!

My life always felt more complete when my big brother was in it. I enjoyed this day with his family so much! The ride home was filled with talk of the wonders that we had seen and then songs to fill the moments until we were home. Eileen had a great singing voice and, having grown up on the prairies, she had learned how to fill the quiet hours with happy songs and games. We were home much quicker than the drive there had seemed! It's strange how the passage of time seems to be effected by moods.

# Chapter 34

Mum had dinner all prepared for us. Roast beef, gravy, Yorkshire pudding, green beans, mashed turnip and carrots, and oven-roasted potatoes! Lynn, Michael and Scott were not here for dinner tonight so Jennifer, Valerie and I could fit at the big table. We spoke about the Enchanted Forest, Dad talked about the television repair calls he did that day, and Mum told Pat that an old friend of his had called and left his number so Pat could call him back. Also, Mum had gone through some old photos today and would like Pat to look at some of them with her after dinner.

We decided to have dessert later as we were all too full for it now. Corinne and I cleared the table while Mum put the food away, Eileen ran a bath for the girls again and then would be putting them to bed as they were both so tired. Edward went to the basement to finish some work on his bench and Pat went to look at the pictures.

There was a lot of memorabilia in the drawer as well as photos. Napkins from special occasions, pieces of wedding cakes from different weddings and newspaper articles. Some of the articles were of my dance shows but, the ones that caught Pat's attention most were of a missing girl from our area! She was 17 and went missing after work at the hotel. It was believed that she would have taken the bus home and would get off just a few blocks from our home. This happened several months ago, and she has not been heard from since. There were four different articles about her in the drawer. Mum came in as Pat was reading one of them.

"Why are these articles here Mum? Did you know her?" asked Pat with concern in his voice. "No, we didn't know her but Edward was concerned because she lives so close and we have girls close to her age," Mum explained. Pat continued reading with a look of concern on his face. "Do you know Mum, this is something that we learn about in crime solving class at the Training Academy. One of the first things they teach us is that the perpetrators of a crime often keep newspaper stories about it, either out of pride or fear of having missed a detail that could convict them."

Mum was only half listening as she was sorting through the old photos of her children when suddenly it hit her what Pat was implying. "Oh Pat, you don't think that Edward could be guilty of this, do you? That's ridiculous!" she replied as she broke into laughter. "Well, I would certainly hope not, but really I don't know Edward very well," he said defensively.

At this point, Edward came in, finished work for the day and wanting to get showered before bed. "Let's ask him, personally. Right now," Pat added looking at Edward. "Oh, come on, that's going too far," protested Mum. "What's going on?" asked Edward. "I want to ask you why you've saved all of these articles about the missing girl?" Pat inquired of Edward. "Oh that, I was just concerned because we have two daughters close to her age and if we know anything about it maybe we could help the police catch the guy." Edward replied. "Well do you know anything about it?" Insisted Pat. "Of course not! I just thought maybe one of us might have seen her or something," stammered Edward, not really seeming offended by being suspected, but fighting to stay in control of himself or the situation. "So, you had no connection to her?" Said Pat wanting a definite answer, so he could put the thought of this out of his mind forever. "Well I had given her a ride home before from work, but not the day she went missing," responded Edward. "What! You never told me that?" answered Mum with a stunned expression. "Oh, come on now. You're making far too much out of this. I had recognized her walking to the bus stop, in the rain downtown. I knew she lived close to our house, as I had repaired her Mother's TV before. I offered her a ride, as a good neighbor and nothing more," insisted Edward in a tone to end the conversation.

Corinne and I were finished the dishes and were getting ready for bed. We did not know about Pat and Edward's discussion but could feel an air of tension when we said goodnight to everyone.

Chapter 35

The next morning began with another great breakfast. This time we had hash browns, fried eggs, bacon, baked beans and toast. "I need to go into town for about an hour for some last-minute Christmas shopping," Eileen mentioned while we were eating, "Do you ladies need anything?" "Yes, I need two more gifts. I was waiting for my allowance from today to be able to get them," I admitted somewhat embarrassed that I had left it to the last minute.

"I could use a few minutes to finish my gift list," Corinne added. "Well, I think we three ladies should go to the mall right after making our beds. We'll finish our shopping and then come and get Jennifer, Valerie and Pat, as we are invited to Lynn and Michael's for dinner tonight. Your Mum, Dad and Scott are invited too but they will go a little later than us.

"We want to come too," shouted Jennifer and Valerie. "I need you little ladies to help me wrap some gifts while your Mum goes shopping," whispered Pat. "Then we'll all go to Auntie Lynn's and Uncle Michael's." "No, I go with Mummy," shouted Valerie in exasperation. "Now, now Valerie, we talked about this. Remember sometimes Mum has to do things alone but Dad and Jennifer will be with you and I will be back soon," Eileen explained lovingly hugging Valerie all the while. "Come on Val, let's go get started so we can be done when Mum gets home," coaxed Pat.

Corinne and I hurried off to make our beds and get ready so we could sneak away quickly before Valerie got upset again. Minutes later we were in the car. It seemed so strange to have Eileen driving, as we had never been with a woman driving before. Our Mother had never learned, Lynn was now driving their car but we had not ridden with her yet. "Please forgive Valerie's crying, she has always only had me to care for her and she still is a little timid to be without me," Eileen told us, although it was not necessary.

Soon we were parked in the stores parkade. "Will you be okay to shop together if I meet you back here in an hour?" asked Eileen. "Sure, we'll be fine" answered Corinne. Eileen disappeared in an instant. "Okay, Tink, let's go to the housewares department so I can buy Mum some oven mitts. Have you thought about what you will buy her?" Corinne asked me.

I hadn't really thought about it because I didn't know how much things cost. I only had $6.41 to buy Edward a licorice pipe, Scott a 45rpm record and something special for Mum. I would just see what I could find.

While Corinne was looking in the housewares department for oven mitts I saw the perfect thing! There was a package of 4 little egg cozies. They were so cute and would sit on top of a boiled egg just like a tea cozy. I lifted up the package and was happy to see the price was just $1.50. I ran with the package to where Corinne was waiting in line to pay for the oven mitts.

"Look I found what I want to buy Mum," I shouted, about to burst with excitement. "Good that you found something but you can't cut into the line, you will have to go and wait at the end," scolded Corinne. "Oh, that's okay, she can go in front of me," said the lady behind Corinne. "I don't think she could stand to wait to buy something so nice for her Mum." The lady added with a twinkle in her eye and a slight chuckle in her voice.

From there we went to the record department where I bought a Righteous Brother's 45rpm for Scott at $1.05. Corinne bought a 45rpm for her friend and an Elvis LP for Scott. We still had 20 minutes left before we had to meet Eileen so we hurried to the candy department for Edward's licorice. They had the black pipes that he liked, 2 for 50 cents. I bought him two pipes and two cigars for $1.04. I still had about $3.00 left so I bought a 25-cent chocolate bar each for Lynn, Michael, Eileen, Pat, Jennifer and Valerie. That way I had something to wrap for everyone. Corinne bought a small box of chocolates for Lynn and Michael and a little bigger one for Pat's family. After paying for our treasures it was almost time to meet Eileen so we rushed back to the parkade. We had just arrived when Eileen appeared with many parcels.

"Good for you girls to be back in time. Did you finish all of your shopping?" Eileen said in excited animation. Seeing us nodding in answer she added, "Well, we will be right on time then, to go back to your house, get dressed for Lynn and Michael's and be there in plenty of time to visit."

We did exactly those things and were soon in the township just outside our city, where Lynn and Michael rented a little two-bedroom bungalow. The first to meet us at the front door were Lynn, her German shepherd puppy, Lady and kitten, Fluffy. "All right you guys, now that you have met our guests I think it's a good time for the both of you to go play in the back yard," Lynn said as she opened the back door and the two animals disappeared like smoke in the wind!

After dinner, the women and girls cleared the tables, the men folded and put away the two card tables into and carried the main table back into the kitchen. Lynn, Mum and Eileen put the food away, Edward started washing the dishes and we girls started drying them and putting them away. Michael went out to feed the animals and he brought wood back in with him to start a fire. His Dad and Scott brought in a keyboard and four poles. It was an organ, and once it was in the house they screwed in the four poles which were its legs.

Within 30 minutes the house was filled with Christmas music, the lights on the tree were on and a warm flickering fire was dancing in the hearth. When everyone was sitting in the living room, Michael brought the animals into the kitchen, but it wasn't long before they too were in the living room. Fluffy spotted a red ball that had fallen from the tree and he and the dog started batting it back and forth. They were so cute that we all watched them. One time she batted the ball right into the fireplace. There was no screen in front of it, so the ball rolled right inside. Fluffy would have gone in after it but Lady jumped in the way to stop her! It all had happened so fast and the ball melted instantly! Thank goodness for Lady or it could have ended the evening on a bad note.

Instead the music played on, and Michael brought out a new game for Corinne and I to play, Ouija. It is a fortune telling game which two people place their fingertips on the Ouija game piece and ask questions. The game piece moves across the lettered and numbered board and spells out your answer. Everyone thought that Corinne and I were pushing the piece to where we wanted it to go. We really were not. They asked a question that we would not know the answer to. The question was how old was Michael's Dad. Being two young girls at eleven and fifteen we really had no idea. Corinne thought maybe 55 and I guessed 60. The game answered 42 and everyone said that was correct. Then we were all spooked and quickly put the game away.

Lynn brought out an incredible Angel Food cake with jelly filling and whipping cream for icing. We each had a piece, the adults had tea or coffee and it was a great ending to a fun day. Tomorrow would be Christmas!! I was so excited, too excited to sleep, but that was okay because I had to wrap the gifts I had bought before I could go to bed anyway. Eileen wanted Jennifer and Valerie to get right to bed so they wouldn't be too tired to enjoy tomorrow. The girls were both so excited and worried that Santa wouldn't be able to find them so far away from home. Eileen assured them that she had sent a letter to Santa explaining everything and Santa wouldn't let them down.

They were still whining until Pat said, "How about if Dad reads you The Night Before Christmas story that I used to read to my little brother and sisters on Christmas Eve."

That settled the girls quietly into their beds with Pat sitting between them. I called down the hall, "Can you leave the door open so we can listen too?" Corinne and I had all the rolls of Xmas wrap, the tape, scissors, gift tags, bows and our newly bought packages to be wrapped all set on the dining room table. It was such a warm finish to a great Christmas Eve!

Chapter 36

The morning came quickly. We opened our stockings in the bedroom to let the adults sleep a little longer. It was so much fun all being together, okay in our pajamas, opening our special packages from Santa. How does he know just what each of us would like? I knew the truth about Santa now but it was still fun to play along.

The joy of being together mattered the most to me. It wasn't long before the younger girls couldn't wait anymore and went to wake their parents. Mum came out of her bedroom dressed in her morning robe, so Corinne and I wore ours for this special day. I felt a little uncomfortable, not being totally dressed with Dad around but soon forgot about it with the Christmas excitement! We each took a seat in the living room while Scott passed out the gifts from under the tree. He gave Mum the gift from me. I was so excited as she unwrapped it.

"These are adorable!" she chuckled as she held them up for all to see. "Thank-you so much, Hanna. They will help to keep the eggs warm until you guys get to the table in the morning."

I opened a box from Scott. An ornament set of little dogs. There was one large dog and five little ones all joined together with a delicate chain. They were so cute. I would name them Mum, Pat, Lynn, Scott, Corinne and Hanna. The next gift I opened was from Corinne. It was a china Mother and child skunk coin bank. I loved them both. We continued opening gifts until the morning was almost gone.

Mum cooked up a great brunch of pancakes, hash brown potatoes, bacon, sausages, fried eggs and toast. After eating our fill, we kids went in the living room and shared in playing with the Spirograph that I had been given by Pat and Eileen, the Topple game that Jennifer and Valerie got from Santa and the Twister game I got from Santa. The hours passed by easily, I didn't even see when Lynn and Michael had arrived. The adults spent a long time drinking tea and coffee at the table in quiet conversation, at least until Pat again mentioned the newspaper clippings of the missing girl.

"Oh, would you get off of that subject!" Edward's raised and agitated voice rang out. "I told you that I just kept them out of concern for my own daughters. I had fixed her Mother's TV and given the girl a lift home, so I felt that I knew her a little. Sorry I cared!"

"No need to get hot under the collar." replied Pat calmly. "In my line of work, I am paid to be curious. I'm sure you've heard the expression 'Thou dost protest too much' well that's what made me ask again." Totally annoyed Edward said, "I can't sit around all day, I have work to do." He got up from the table and headed down to his workshop.

Pat left the table as well and came into the living room saying, "Well ladies this is our last day here so what shall we do? It's so nice out, compared to Saskatchewan weather, shall we go down to the park and feed the ducks?" I was again struck with that ominous foreboding feeling! "It's not your last day here?" slipped from my lips. "Well yeah, it is Tink. We will have breakfast together tomorrow, but then we must be underway to catch the 10 o'clock ferry." Pat informed us like he was reading the morning paper or even worse the funny papers, with a light heartedness to his voice. He didn't realize that my life was slipping down my legs and away as he spoke, like sand in an hour-glass. I felt hollow and empty. The tears wanted to spill from my eyes but I was trying to hold them back to keep from embarrassing myself. Pat had his own family now and they had come to share him with us, it was now time for them to go.

I could not hide the look of distress though and Pat saw it. He came and put his arm around me saying soothingly, "Come on Kerr. Don't take it so hard, we'll be back, or you can come and stay with us sometime." His closeness only released the floodgate of tears and I tried so hard to pull myself together. "Come on Tink. We've still got today and some of tomorrow. Let's not waste it crying," urged Corinne who often helped to pull me back together.

"Okay. I'll go get washed and dressed for the park," I answered.

The six of us: Pat, Eileen, Corinne, Jennifer, Valerie and I had a great couple of hours in the fresh air on a crisp, Christmas Day afternoon.

We fed the ducks a whole loaf of marked down bread that we bought at the corner store. We hiked up the hill and viewed the beautiful ocean. Then we finished off with rides on the garden swings where you could sit across from your partner and while away the hours. Today there were only moments as we had to get home for a family dinner.

As soon as we were out of the car, we could smell the delicious aroma of roast beef. Edward had set up the barbeque just outside the kitchen door, with a huge roast on a skewer, rotating over the hot coals. Inside Lynn and Mum had prepared potato salad, green salad, hot dinner buns and corn nib lets, as corn on the cob cannot be found in winter.

"Wow, a summer feast! It's so beautiful outside it almost feels like summer to us poor prairie folk. I guess when we get home we'll be greeted with snow and wind chill factors for the next 3 or 4 months yet!" announced Pat. "Well, we didn't want to give you turkey again," replied Mum, with a twisted face as she was getting a squeeze from Pat.

We enjoyed a great meal, all together in the dining room. It would be quite a while before we were all together again. There was even apple pie with ice cream for dessert. We lingered around the table after the dinner was done. Then Eileen got the girls into the tub for a bath before bed, while she packed away all the clothes they would not wear tomorrow. Pat started taking out the packed cases to arrange them in the car, some going under the plywood bed on the back seat, where people's feet would go if they were sitting on the regular seat. He checked the oil and water in the engine and the supplies in his emergency kit. By the time he was done, Eileen had the girls tucked nicely into bed. Mum had made tea for the adults and I was having my bath.

It was a very uncomfortable time for me. It was almost hard to breath, as if a weight was on my chest. Did anyone else feel like me? Once dried and in my nightie, I went to say goodnight. I just waved at the end of the hallway, as I felt vulnerable in my pajamas. I lay awake until well after Corinne came in from her shower, dreading saying good-bye in the morning. I did manage to sleep, somehow, because I awoke to Eileen waking her girls to get dressed. Corinne and I dressed to come up with them.

In the kitchen, Mum had prepared coffee, tea and cereal or toast for the travelers. No one else felt like eating. Edward was talking with

Pat about which route they were going to take through the mountains. That didn't matter to me, how they were going, I just wished that I was going too.

"Well, ladies, I guess we better get a move on," Pat motioned his family towards the door. We all followed. Mum and Edward said good-bye at the door. Scott had already gone to work early this morning so had said good-bye last night. Corinne and I followed them to their car. I tried so hard not to cry. I was still in control while I hugged Jennifer, Valerie, and Eileen but, as soon as Pat gave me his big bear hug, I turned into a sobbing puddle of Jell-O.

"Come on Kerr, you'll see us again. Maybe you can even come and stay with us in the summer." Pat tried to reassure me. "I know," I muttered between sobs. "Come on, Tink. We've got to let them go," said Corinne replacing her arms around me letting Pat pull his away. We waved until their car was out of sight, then we ran inside to look out the dining room window until we saw their car drive down the highway across the inlet. We went back to my room. Corinne gathered all of her things to take back to her room. Then we took the sheets and blankets from Pat, Eileen's, Jennifer's and Valerie's beds and put them in the laundry hamper.

"Scott and Dad will take the rental beds apart tonight and Dad will take them back tomorrow," said Mum trying to fill the emptiness that surrounded us now, with words.

Corinne had plans to go out with some friends at one o'clock so she hurried to put clean sheets on her bed. Then she took her things out of my room and put them back into hers. She had to run the vacuum cleaner through the living room, dining room and hallway. This she did with ease, anything to leave on time. I just felt hollow, like the tin man on The Wizard of Oz. I'm sure that if you knocked on my chest it would echo, as did the Tin Man's. I had no ambition, purpose or dreams. I just whiled away the hours, then days, then weeks turning into months. The only hobbies I truly enjoyed were dancing and Girl Guides.

Chapter 37

February held some excitement. The Girl Guides hosted a dance. It was to teach us etiquette and manners. The Scout troop, who used our hall on Tuesday nights, was invited to our dance. I felt very nervous, as it was my first dance with boys. A few different boys asked me to dance, I was sure that they were told to. Then one particular boy asked me again and then didn't want me to sit down between dances. I was sure that everyone was talking about us! Then our captain, the guide leader, blew the whistle, announcing time for revelry, the end of our meeting.

When we broke up into our sixers groups as always for revelry, some of the older girls asked, "Why were you dancing with Ronald, Hanna? He's such a loser!" "He asked me to dance, so I was dancing," I said blushing. "Just because he asked you, doesn't mean you can't say no. Have some pride." Carol snapped at me. I don't know why she thought he was a loser. He seemed quite nice looking to me and we didn't have enough time to talk and get to know each other. Besides I thought that I was more a loser than he was. Nothing more was said about this and I never saw that boy again.

My Dance Troupe had a show booked at the Playhouse in Victoria for May 10 and 11th. This took all of my attention! I was to be in 2 dances. One was a Hawaiian dance. My costume was a cotton shift of bright fuchsia flowers. With this we wore flowered wristbands, anklet and a ring of flowers on our heads. The dance was done kneeling, facing a partner, with a puelly stick (this is a bamboo stick about 16" long with the top 14" cut in long strips about 1/4" wide so that these 10 or 12 strips would rattle when banged together.) It is truly a Hawaiian folk dance. The second dance I was in was the finale. There were 14 of us, all dressed in light blue, stretchy, snug bathing suits with shoulders and cap sleeves. Across our chest was a Canadian flag and at our tummies, following the leg edge of the bathing suit, was a V shape of 3" white fringe. In our hair, we wore a band of blue feathers to match our blue suits. It was actually looked quite impressive with our white tap shoes. We did patterns and routines ending in a chorus line, with linked arms, doing high kicks. What a great experience!! These memories would help hold me on through my many years of being unable to dance.

The month of June was filled with the usual school exams, this time to pass grade 6. I was promoted to grade seven. School ended that year quite uneventfully. Soon summer days passed by wastefully. I had taken a babysitting course to get a Guide "child keeping badge" that spring so, when Corinne got a part time job that summer, she referred all of her babysitting clients to me. I remember this one family of three kids who were always in bed when I got to their house. They had a huge ginger cat. I was watching TV, sitting in their nice lounger with my feet on the footstool, when the cat came in the room and jumped onto my lap! It must have weighed 35 lbs.! There was no way I could move it and my body vibrated with its purring! I was embarrassed to be awakened by the parents calling to me when they arrived home at 3:30 A.M. That was the last time I let myself fall asleep while babysitting. I think it was also the last time I sat for that family.

Their neighbors also had two little boys and a baby girl who I sat for. The third time I went there I could sense something had happened. Maybe they had some bad news or a disagreement or something but you could feel the tension in the air. When the Mum said goodnight to the boys and asked them to get into bed, the eldest boy complied. The younger boy seemed upset about something though, and wanted to wait for his dad first. When the dad came in the kitchen, this son pulled open the silverware drawer and screaming, started throwing knives and forks all around. The more the dad tried to get control, the worse the situation got. Finally, I said, "Maybe you should just go and leave him with me, I'll try to calm him down."

The Mum was already in the car and, because I don't think the Dad knew what else to do, he agreed and they left. They yelled to me, over the noise of falling cutlery, that they would call when they got to their meeting to be sure that the son had calmed down. It was a frightening experience for me at eleven. I did not want the boy to hurt either himself or me with the implements and he would not stop when asked. So, dodging the weapons, I got a hold of the boy. He was strong enough with his rage to continue his onslaught. I was forced to pull him to the floor. I straddled over him with my legs to hold him still, but he struggled on. I spoke to him quietly, trying to sooth him. I asked him if he wanted to tell me why he was so angry, maybe I could help him. He never spoke but his breathing slowed and his body relaxed. I offered to let him go if he would just go to his bed like his Mum had wanted. He did not respond but as soon as I lifted my weight from him he bolted to his bed. I gave him a moment and then went to check on him. He and his brother were both already asleep in their bunk beds with the light on. I switched the light off, waiting to see if this disturbed them. When it didn't, I went to check their little sister. She too was sound asleep in her crib. Looking in from the outside, this would seem like the ideal family! They had a cozy three, bedroom bungalow with a beautiful living room, dining room and family room. A husband, wife and three adorable children but all was not as it seemed. Something dreadful was underlying it and the children were aware of it. Yes, the parents did phone to check if all was well and they were thankful that they could now enjoy their meeting. I worried for the boy and the whole family.

I spent my summer doing morning chores and the afternoons were my own. Sometimes I chose to bake or I played Barbies with friends, some days I would just ride my bike. One day I was at the park and Wesley Foster came and talked to me on the swings for about an hour.

My birthday would be in a couple of days, I would be turning 12. That was always the signal that summer was almost over. We were just going to have a barbeque dinner with Mum, Dad, Lynn and Michael, Scott and Lori, Corinne, Donna and myself. Donna would sleep over. I did look forward to going back to school this year. My friends and I would be grade seven, the seniors of elementary school. Donna and I spent most of that night talking about what it might be like.

Chapter 38

The first day of school was always very exciting, seeing how the kids had changed over the summer. Everyone was wearing new clothes for the first day or two. Carrying my new school supplies, I noticed there were more items for grade seven. It made me feel that there would be more expected from me this year.

We stood in the courtyard and waited for our names to be called to see whose class we would be in, with what kids and what teacher. Finally, my name was called. I was a little scared as I didn't know many of the kids in my class very well and we had a new teacher to our school, Mr. Mackrae. He was dressed very nicely and spoke with a deep, clear voice. I hoped he couldn't see how timid I felt having a man for a teacher again.

The first few weeks seemed to go well in class. Mr. Mackrae had certain ideas of how he liked his classroom organized and we arranged our desks accordingly. He told us how much homework we could be expected to turn in each morning and how many assignments we would have throughout the year. I knew he meant it when he said that we would have to keep our noses to the grindstone to do well in his class.

I actually felt exhilarated by the challenge and was listening intently as he was explaining a difficult math principle when things suddenly changed. I had my elbow bent on my desk, with my head rested on my hand trying to follow every word he said. Suddenly he slammed the huge book he was holding shut!!! Lowering his deep voice, but raising its volume, he shouted, "Why am I wasting my time with you inconsiderate people? Darlene, Yvonne and Hanna get out of here and wait in the hall for me!"

I started searching the faces in the room, was there another Hanna? "Never mind trying to act surprised! I know your type, trying to act all sweet and nice! Get out as you've been told before I consider the

151

strap!" boomed his voice behind me as somehow my legs carried me from the room.

In the hallway, stood Darlene and Yvonne looking as angry as Mr. Mackrae. "This is going to be some year with this jerk!" huffed Darlene. "Why are "you" out here?" asked Yvonne looking at me. I did not want to answer lest I got in more trouble. I felt that I would either wet my pants or vomit, my legs collapsing under me. I had never been so afraid before.

The classroom door opened just then and Mr. Mackrae stepped into the hall and shut the door behind him. "Do you three girls think I come here to school just to waste my time?" he snarled looking down at us. "Well?" Darlene and Yvonne just glared back at him as he focused on each of us. "No sir," I answered as he looked at me, my voice quivering. "Then why weren't you paying attention instead of nodding off?" he snapped at me. As if I wasn't mortified enough now I started to cry as I answered, "No sir, I wasn't sleeping, my head just gets heavy when I am really trying to understand something that is so hard."

I think Mr. Macrae thought I was telling the truth, "Alright, you go to the washroom and wash your face and then wait for me in the cloakroom," he told me. I did as I was instructed. On my way back to the cloakroom, I walked by the office and I heard Darlene and Yvonne getting the strap. I wondered if that would happen to me in the cloakroom. I waited as I was told but could hear all of the kids talking about me in the classroom. I wanted to sit down but there was nowhere in the cloakroom to sit.

Soon the door opened and Mr. Macrae came in. "Now explain to me again why you were sleeping?" he demanded. "Sir, I wasn't sleeping," I explained as the tears started flowing again. "All right, let's step in here while we talk," he said opening the storage closet that he kept extra papers in. I was afraid to step into the little 5'x3' room but knew I had no choice. He stepped in with me, shutting the door behind us. "Now explain," he said. "When I am trying to understand something that is really difficult my head just gets too heavy for my neck to hold. I was supporting my head on my hand while I was trying to follow your explanation. I wasn't falling asleep, sir." I tried to tell him again between the hiccups caused by my tears.

"Okay," he said handing me a Kleenex, "Dry up those tears, then come back into class." He opened the storage closet door and stepped out, shutting the door behind him. I started drying my tears thinking, "Phew, I didn't get the strap!" From then on, I would always be nervous because I would never know when my world could explode for no reason. When I opened the door, and slunk back to my desk, I could feel every kid's eyes upon me. I didn't like it and I felt uglier than ever.

Things calmed down after that day. It wasn't until after our first report card that my Mother had an interview with Mr. Mackrae. He said to her, "I misjudged Hanna early on in the year. Most children would have rebelled out of anger, but Hanna amazed me by staying true to her course and proving me wrong. I really respect her for that." I however lost respect for him, that he never told me that himself, when I needed to hear it so badly!

At school in November, our language class was divided into three groups according to our marks. One group would focus in on spelling. The next group would concentrate on adjectives, nouns, etc. and the final group would do a play! I was lucky to be in this group. There was a new girl in our class, her name was Lily. She was tall, blonde, beautiful and popular already, she asked if we could write our own play.

"That would make it a much larger challenge," pondered Mr. Mackrae. "I believe maybe this group could handle that. It has to be written and performed by December 14th. Do you think you could manage that?" "Sure, we can," answered Lily, the only one of us who was sure. "We'll start today after class and meet every day we need to until it's done."

The nine of us did meet after school that day. Janet, Donna, Lily, Sandra, Bob, Ronald, Murray, Douglas, all of the smart kids in my class, and me. "The first thing to do is think of what kind of play we want to do" said Lily standing tall and confident. "I think we should make it a comedy, everybody likes those," offered Murray. "Yeah!" chimed in the other boys. "We could make it in an operating room like on all those soap operas," suggested Sandra.

"Well let's go home for today and think about it, as it's getting late. Tomorrow bring in any props you might use in an operating room and we'll get started," instructed Janet.

"Oh, my gosh, it is four o'clock already, my Mum will be worried and I will be in trouble!" I exclaimed as I hurried all the way home. I arrived home at 4:30, physically tired but my mind churning with ideas for the play. I had no idea about what the script could be but I had lots of props from my old doctor's kit.

"Sorry I'm late, Mum. I was chosen by Mr. Mackrae to be in a play in my Language class and we had to meet after school. We will probably be late everyday now until Christmas as there is a lot to do." I babbled on and on, too excited. Dinner was ready so we sat down right away to eat. Corinne wasn't home again as she was staying over at Gloria's. This was a real bone of contention between Corinne and my Mum. After dinner, I cleared the table dishes into the dishwasher. Then I did my Arithmetic homework, watched Jackie Gleason with my parents, had a bath and went to bed, reading my library book for my book report on Friday.

Classes the next day dragged by, as I was waiting for the play meeting after school. "Did everyone remember to bring props?" inquired Ronald. Everyone did have something, from real stethoscopes (two people's fathers were doctors) to hot water bottles, tongue depressors and ice bags. You name it, we had it. This was going to be fun! Today there was just time to organize the props, tonight we would start to think about the script!

I arrived home at about the same time as yesterday. Mum wasn't happy about me staying so late as it was dark. "Well I walked with Donna, so at least I wasn't alone." I told Mum and she did feel somewhat better knowing that. Donna and I both had dancing together on Wednesday evenings from 6-8 and Saturdays from 12-3. Then we had Girl Guides on Thursdays from 6-8:30. The playgroup met every day after school for an hour but excused Donna and I on Wednesdays and Thursdays. It seemed the busier I was away from home, the more Corinne stayed at Gloria's.

My Mum was getting ill at this time. She would always go to bed directly from the dinner table and, often, couldn't even make dinner. Sometimes Dad would fry eggs with toast and baked beans for dinner. On the weekends, I would cook pork chops or a casserole to freeze and reheat during the week just in case Mum was too ill to cook.

The days had been speeding past, with my playgroup always meeting and having a great time. The entire play was written and we practiced it, laughing the whole time. I had never seen an operating room in a soap opera but I believed the others had, and that this is what it was like.

154

Our actors, playing doctors joked all the way through the scenes. We had all written our own jokes and we thought they were so funny, at least until the afternoon of December 14th when we performed the play in front of the whole school. It was the longest 8 minutes of my life! There was almost no laughter from the audience. Each time one of the actors said something we had thought was hilarious, nothing happened, except that our faces got redder and redder.

The play ended. We lined up across the front of the stage holding hands and bowing to an audience that looked perplexed. They didn't even know that our play was over, or that what they had seen was even a play. At first only the teachers were applauding! Then the teachers stood clapping in front of their classes and the kids clapped as well. The nine of us went back stage, dying of embarrassment! We could hear the audience leaving to go back to their classes. Finally, somebody spoke. Bob said what we all were thinking, "What happened?"

Mr. Mackrae walked in just in time to hear it. We all thought that we were in big trouble!

"I'm sure that this reaction to your play is quite a shock to all of you. This has been a very good, but difficult lesson for all of you. Comedy is said to be in the eye of the beholder, this play is proof of that. You all had such a good time doing this play and you thought that it was funny. Sitting on the outside looking in, as the audience was, is a different story. Perhaps they could not see things as well or hear things as you could? From their perspective, the humor was lost. For your letter grade on this project, I am sure you will be surprised that I will give each of you an A." An audible gasp went up in the room followed by creased foreheads and confused looks. "I thought you would be shocked. I know how hard each of you worked on this project. How many hours of your time and energy you used. Maybe the audience didn't laugh as you had expected but you have all learned an invaluable lesson. You learned about pride, humility, perseverance, research, time management and, what I am most proud of you all for, is that none of you quit when the going got tough! You each carried on with your lines, supporting your fellow actors. You should all be very proud of yourselves for this, as I am of you," said Mr. Mackrae making eye contact with each of us. Once again, he had brought me to tears but this time they were tears of relief and joy. "It's just about time for the bell to ring for the end of the day. Please gather your things, congratulate each other on your performances and say good-bye until Monday." "Thank-you Mr. Mackrae! You touched my heart in such a personal way! I will never forget it!" I thought to myself.

Chapter 39

Only 9 days until Christmas. Donna and I wanted to buy each other a friendship ring for Christmas. We took the bus together for the first time without a parent, or in my case an older sibling. We got off of the bus in front of the department store. We felt so mature walking into the store together, without an adult. We headed straight for the jewelry counter. There were many styles of friendship rings to choose from, as they were quite the rage at the time. We decided on two matching gold bands with raised, vertical stripes every 1/16 of an inch around the band. At the time, we believed them to be pure gold for $1.05 each, plus tax. We had just enough of our saved allowances left to go upstairs for a coke and a shared plate of French fries! This was such a special thing for us near teens. Then it was time to catch the bus home before dark.

We were waiting for the bus that serviced the route to our area, the city transit buses didn't travel out as far as our road. The buses to our area weren't always very dependable and this was one of those times. The schedule showed that it would pick up at the mall at 4:20 P.M., we had been waiting since 4:10 and it was now 5:05 and still no bus! Another transit bus came that would stop close to our neighborhood.

I said, "Don, I think we should take this bus. It will mean a mile long walk home but we will at least get there. I don't trust the other bus to come at all." Donna agreed and we boarded the bus for the half hour ride to near home. It was just starting to get dark now and the dusk gave an eerie look to everything we saw. Everything looked foreign. Nothing along the route looked familiar until, about ten minutes later, we finally recognized the area near where they were building the new Junior High School that we would attend next year. A moment later we reached the Bakery. I remembered it from picking Corinne up at the bus stop before.

It was the last stop the bus made before turning around for the trip back into town. Donna and I disembarked, thanking the driver, and stepped down the stairs into the darkness outside. It seemed amplified by contrast to the bus's lit interior. Donna and I each grabbed for the other's hand for courage as we marched defiantly home.

I could see across the road was the home of the Strable family. I had waited there in Scott's car once when he had run in to get something from his friend, Lee. I had sat there longingly hoping that Lee's younger brother, Mark, would come out and talk to me. I had seen him there before and I thought he looked just like the cute boy that played the rifleman's son on TV. He didn't appear, which was probably lucky for me as I don't know what I would have done if he did.

Suddenly a terrible screaming sound pierced the darkness! It was like the noises Indians made while attacking in the Roy Roger's Show. Don and I started to run for home, terrified. We were running by our school, when we saw a group of boys there, riding their bikes and we realized they were making the noise. We stopped running immediately so we wouldn't seem so immature as to be afraid of the dark. One of the boys started to ride toward us. It was Bob, he and his family were good friends of Donna's and her family. Some of the boys followed Bob. In a moment, Don and I were encircled by boys on their bikes. It was a pleasant feeling to have gotten their attention, although I knew they were only there because of Donna, it had nothing to do with me. She was quite pretty and petite while I felt that I was tall and gangly. She was involved with a number of clubs at school so she always had things to talk about with the boys. I felt inept as I had no hobbies other than dancing and Guides, both of which held no interest for boys.

"What brings you over here?" Bob asked Donna. "Hanna and I just caught the bus home from the Mall," Donna answered. Larry Hampton was a new guy to our neighborhood. He was bigger than most of the boys, maybe a little older too, and a bit of a Hippy. He said "So what was so exciting at the mall to attract you two ladies?" "We wanted to buy our Christmas presents for each other," I replied. Chuckling, teasingly Larry added, "So is it a big surprise now until Christmas or can you tell us what you bought?" The tone of Donna's reply told me she didn't really like Larry when she snapped, "It's none of your business!"

I felt embarrassed for Larry. I apologetically bent my wrist up just enough to raise my hand by my side and said, "We bought these matching friendship rings." The gold sparkle on my finger really looked quite impressive to me. I really thought it was gold and not just the painted plastic that it was. Donna looked at me, a little disappointed that I had shown him, but still accepting of my soft heartedness. She knew me well, I would spare anyone's feelings.

"Hell, does this mean that you're married to each other? Lesbians! Oh, Sandy you'll be so disappointed!" Larry said with total disregard for our feelings. "Get lost!" Sandy shouted at Larry. Then he muttered something under his breath to the rest of the guys. Donna and I resumed our fast-paced walk home. We knew our families would be worried about us, out almost an hour past dark. We still had a good half mile to go and were quite relieved when Bob and Sandy came on their bikes saying, "We'll ride with you to your house since it's so dark."

We didn't talk much though as we saved our energy for the brisk pace. Bob did tell us that his family was going to have a neighborhood pre-Christmas party and that we were all welcome to come. We had made good time walking home and were already walking past the park on our road when a voice yelled out of the dark, "What the hell's going on here?" Stepping a bit closer, I saw that it was Edward. "Oh, it's okay guys, it's my Dad," I sighed in relief but I was ashamed to have to admit he was a member of my family. He had shouted with such a vile, suspicion filled voice. I worried what my friends would think of him.

"I better hurry in. Thanks guys for accompanying us safely home," offered Donna as she dashed into her house. "Do you know your poor Mother has been worrying herself sick while you've been out here doing God knows what with these boys!" raged Edward, further humiliating me. "Excuse me sir, I was just riding home when we saw Hanna and Donna walking the same way. We thought it would be safer if we went together," spoke Bob quite startled and offended at having to justify his ride actions. "I'm gonna ride home, Bob," stated Sandy as he spun his bike around giving his head a little shake. "What was he doing here if he doesn't live this way?" asked Edward accusingly, staring poignantly at me. "He was coming to spend the night at my house as we have a karate lesson together in the morning," affirmed Bob looking quite puzzle. "Thanks for getting

159

me home safe, Bob. Good luck on your karate test tomorrow," I said in hopes of excusing Bob before something else embarrassing happened.

"Yeah, goodnight," Bob answered as he popped a wheelie on his bike and sped away home. Marching up my driveway with Edward behind me I feared that he might grab me! He did not touch me but snapped, "We'll see what your Mother has to say about this!"

Climbing the stairs, I felt a combination of happiness at finally being home and dread at what dirty story Edward might turn this situation into. As I turned the knob to open the door, I could see the kitchen table set for dinner. "Mum, I'm home," I announced. She was not in the kitchen but I heard her coming from the bedroom. In a voice filled with fatigue she said, "Thank goodness, at last. Where have you been all this time?" "Donna and I waited at the mall, from 4:10 until after 5 o'clock, but our bus never came. Then the other bus arrived so we thought we better take it. We knew that it would drop us a mile away from home but our bus might never have come. We walked home as fast as we could because we knew that you'd be worried," spilled out of me like water from an overflowing bucket.

"Funny you didn't mention the part about the boys," Edward added accusingly.

Mum looked a little concerned but more baffled at trying to get the story straight. "I was getting to that part," I interjected. "When we walked by the school, Bob and Sandy came along on their bikes. They were riding to Bob's house for the night. Bob started talking with Donna about some schoolwork and before we knew it we were here." "A likely story!" said Edward his voice filled with contempt. "I don't know why you say that, dear? Hanna has never done anything to cause me to be suspicious," was all that Mum said in response. "Let's have our dinner."

Corinne and Scott were both out for the evening, so it was just the three of us at the dinner table. This added to the air of discomfort. I felt anxious about what my friends would think of my family. Edward appeared to be uncomfortable because he felt my Mum had been fooled by me. Mum was just disappointed that the dinner was a little dry from waiting in the oven so long. There was very little conversation.

Mum did ask me, "Did you find what you went to the mall for?" "Oh yes," I said as I held up my hand to show her my ring. Somehow it didn't seem as special anymore. Soon I excused myself to go wash the "hand dishes", the pots and pans that didn't go in the dishwasher. In the meantime, Mum scraped their dishes and loaded them into the dishwasher. She said, "Goodnight," to me then headed off to her bed. She never felt very well these days and a lot was blamed on the traumatic experiences she had while delving into her past with my real father at the psychiatrist's office. She never spoke of her episodes to us. We all just felt that it was only her business.

I lay awake in bed for hours thinking about the day and feeling embarrassed. Soon I heard Corinne come home and I thought it was too bad that we didn't still share our room so I could tell her about my day. I did not know that she was still constantly accusing Edward of somehow spying on her.

Chapter 40

The next morning, we were to do extra cleaning to get ready for Christmas. It didn't seem as exciting because Pat, Eileen and the girls couldn't come home this year. Still, we did our cleaning and the smell of Christmas baking filled the air. Scott had gone to buy our tree today and, after it stood overnight in the stand, we would decorate it tomorrow. This would be our last tree together!

I awoke that morning to the sound of Christmas carols from the stereo. Elvis Presley singing I'll be home for Christmas. It made me think of Pat, who wouldn't be home this Christmas, so I began the day crying quietly into my pillow.

Everyone had plans for the afternoon, so our tree decorating had to be done right after breakfast. It started with Scott putting on the lights. Trying to keep the festive feeling he sang, "Jingle Bells," "Joy to the world", and "We three Kings" all within three-minutes. He always made me laugh! Scott was booked to paint his bosses guest house today, ready for Christmas company. So, he had no time to waste.

Corinne and I hung the Garland, Candy canes, festively wrapped chocolates, colored balls and bells and last but not least the icicles. At 12 o'clock Corinne announced, "I have to go. You can finish though, can't you?" looking at me with her eyes pleading. Sure I could, it was Christmas, and I knew she must have good reason to go. I continued hanging icicles for about another half-hour.

Mum came into the room. "Oh, that is beautiful!", she exclaimed, "but where is Corinne? She was supposed to be doing this with you!" "Oh, she was, she just left a minute ago." I explained.

"I will never understand that girl" my Mother sighed.

This statement was sadly so true and would remain this way for the rest of their lives. With every misunderstanding, they faced over the years, those words hauntingly whispered in my ears. I felt the pain for each of them because the love was genuinely there, but the connection was not!

Christmas 1967 passed by, with all the usual great meals, gifts, and family time. Only Pat and his family were missing. Grade seven continued after the Christmas break. I swear I had grown 3 inches in height and gained 10 lbs. in weight over those 10 days. I felt like I stuck out like a sore thumb in my classroom. We continued on with the usual school activities of reading writing and arithmetic. In my youth, the days just dragged by and all I lived for was my dancing.

Donna's father had been given a big promotion and they were moving back to Ottawa. She was already excited about the big junior high school that she would be going to. Her family would be leaving on Monday to drive across the country and get set up in their new home.

Suddenly, June was upon us. It was our last year in the elementary school, as long as we passed the subject matter which again was determined by the gauntlet of government exams. After suffering through these, the parents fund raising committee decided it would be a good time to hold a games night. An invitation was sent to the grade eight students from both Junior high schools. Some of the kids in grade 7 would be going to one of these schools next year, depending on which district they lived in. This way they could meet some of the kids they would be going to school with next year. I would be going to the brand, new school and so there was nobody to invite from there.

Games night began at 6 p.m. the last Friday night of elementary school. I walked to school that evening with Shelly, who was my new best friend now that Donna had moved away. She lived 10 minutes from my house and another 10 minutes from the school. We were both excited, and had so much to chat about, that it seemed we were at the school in seconds. The first thing we did was buy a roll of tickets to be used as we chose. The roll cost $2.50.

In one classroom, there was a cakewalk set up. To play here, it cost three tickets or $.75. There were squares of paper with numbers on them, taped to the floor in a circle. To begin, each person who had paid their tickets, stood on a numbered square. When the music started we walked in a circle around the numbers until the music stopped. Then, the person who had collected the money for the tickets, called out a number. If you were standing on that number, you won a cake of your choice from a whole table of beautifully decorated cakes. This was my favorite game but, I played three times, and didn't win a cake.

Another room had a fishing tank in it. Here you paid two tickets or $.50 and you were given a fishing rod. We were told to fish over what looked like a small stage. I caught a small game of checkers. There was also a game of ring toss set up. To play you paid $.50 or two tickets. I tried my luck twice, but I never won at this game either, so didn't see the prizes.

On our way to check out the next game, we ran into a boy that Shelley knew. She introduced me to him saying, "Hi Bart, I wondered if you would be here tonight? I knew the teachers had sent a flyer to your school inviting everyone. Hanna, this is an old friend of my family, his name is Bart."

I thought he was pretty cute, tall and a little older than I was. He was very polite. He responded with a handshake saying, "Good to meet you, Hanna. I would like you to meet my friend, Maurice." I hadn't noticed the tall guy, with shoulder length, blond hair standing beside him. "Hi" was all he said to me and I to him.

The four of us continued on walking to the next game. Shelley and Bart chatted away with each other. Maurice and I followed behind. I know I felt uncomfortable, wishing I knew what to say to a stranger. Then he spoke to me, asking," Is Southland brand-new?" That was the name of the school I'd be going to next year. I answered, "Yes, we will be the first students in that school." "That rocks! You guys are so lucky. Our school is so old, it stinks of mold." he responded.

One classroom was set up as a small café. We headed there to use the last of our tickets, having a hot dog and pop each. From here on in the conversation flowed very easily. At 8:30 we decided to head outside to wait for our ride home. It was Shelley's Mom we were expecting as my Dad had dropped us off.

While we were waiting outside, some other boys arrived at the school and started causing trouble with Bart and Maurice. Suddenly, we were all on the run around the school. It was good exercise but very confusing for me because Maurice and I ended up losing the rest of the group. We decided to wait at the school driveway for them, and Shelley's Mom. I thought that was where she would pick us up because that is where my Dad had dropped us off.

We waited and waited in the freezing cold, sharing one hood and she never came. Finally, the Principal came out and said "Everybody has gone, you guys had better get home." So, we took off running to Shelley's house to see if they might be there already. Boy, did I get in trouble from Shelley's Mom when we arrived. I was very confused as to what I had done wrong but, apparently, the plan was for us all to walk home together. Nobody had told me that!

The first thing Shelley's Mom said to me was "You little Hussy!" I remember wanting to explain to her what had happened but she didn't want to hear anything I had to say.

We decided it was best to get out of there, so Maurice offered to walk me home. We walked to the bottom of my street and then went separate directions, he to the highway to hitchhike home and myself up the street to my house. When I finally arrived home, about 2 hours late, my Mum greeted me with a frantic, angry look on her face. I kind of collapsed onto a chair to explain what had happened. My Mum was horrified that Shelley's Mom had spoken to me like that, and she made me some hot chocolate while I went and got my pajamas on. It sure felt good to get into bed that night but it took a good 3 years to get over the sting of Shelley's Mom's words.

Chapter 41

The next day there was a knock on our door. To my surprise, it was Maurice and his friend Bart. I let them in, showed them around the house and took them downstairs to the rumpus room. We had a pool table down there. We played a game each and then it was time for them to go home. Maurice gave me a quick kiss as they left. My parents hadn't even been home yet. Mum was out getting her hair done and Dad was at work.

The teachers threw us a party for the end of grade 7, as we were leaving elementary school. They held it in the portable attached to the main school building so that we wouldn't disturb the rest of the kids.

That summer, I spent a lot of time with Maurice. He used to come and get me and we would walk all the way up to Thetis lake, walk around the lake and then he would walk me back as far as the highway where we would go separate ways again. We always had so much to talk about during those walks. I told him all about my family, my 4 siblings, my 2 Dads and my Mum. He only had 1 Dad, 1 Mom and an adopted sister. His mother was never very well and giving birth to Maurice had made it impossible for her to have a second baby. We walked so many miles that summer and if I had known then that I would be in a wheelchair someday, I would have been more grateful for each step.

The excitement of starting grade 8 was overwhelming. It would be a brand-new school, not just to me but to the district. It was right on the water that connected to the inlet behind my house. It took me over an hour to walk to school by road but in the winter, when the inlet was frozen and we could walk across it, it only took 20 minutes. It was fun to meet a bunch of new kids and all the new teachers. I enjoyed all the different subjects but English was my favorite.

One September day when I came out of school to head home, Edward was parked out front waiting to pick me up. He honked to get my attention as I didn't know he was coming. I walked over to the car wondering why he was there. He said "I just finished a call and thought I would pick you up on my way by". I was suspicious as to his intentions and my skin started to crawl but I got in the car because he was my Dad.

We drove home, not saying much but he asked how my day had been. The drive was quick and I was glad for it. I got into the house and there was a strange feeling in the air. I knew something was up but had no idea what. Lynn and Michael, Scott and Lori, Corinne and Mum were all there. It wasn't Christmas so it was odd to see everyone together.

We all sat in the living room and Lynn, holding my Mother's hand, spoke the words that my Mother was unable to. She let us know that our father had gone fishing on Nanaimo Lakes, like he always loved to do. This time he was with a lady friend of his, when their boat overturned. The water was freezing cold and my Dad was not a good swimmer. He had probably been drinking as well. The lady was able to swim to shore as soon as the boat overturned and she kept calling for my Dad, wondering where he was. Then she heard him answer and she realized he was clinging to the overturned boat. She was very brave, as her legs were frozen solid, but she still went back to try to save him.

As she reached the boat, my Dad slid under. She was unable to find him under the water, so she had to swim back to shore. The poor woman had to drag herself back through the bushes all the way to someone's house to get help. Her legs were all torn up from the sticks and rocks. Later, when I saw her at his funeral, her legs were still bandaged and healing. You could see a lot of the torn skin showing around the bandages. I know she didn't give up easily when she tried to save him.

My Mum had always asked him not to go fishing when they were married as she knew he didn't swim well but he always went anyway. That night I spent thinking of all the things I did remember about my Dad, it wasn't a whole lot. One special memory was fishing by the river with him when I was 3 or 4.

The next morning, I got up and went to school as usual. As I walked the railroad tracks, I didn't even hear the train whistle until after everyone else had already jumped off the tracks. I got out of the way just in time and all the kids were asking me if I was okay. I had to say "My Dad just died yesterday. I guess I was thinking about him and not about what I am doing".

I got to school and felt like I was moving through a fog. In English class, my teacher noticed I wasn't paying attention and said "Hanna, don't waste my time, if you aren't wanting to learn, leave the class." I looked up from my fog and apologized, saying "My Dad died yesterday and I can't think clearly." The teacher looked astonished and said "I had no idea, we will make sure you get home right away." He arranged to have me go home with a friend. She was very happy to be pulled out of school as well. We had a nice talk all the way home and I got to tell her what little I knew about my Dad.

. . . .

Sadly, Hanna passed away before she was able to finish writing her family story. She was told about a week before she died that her left lung had completely filled with fluid from an infection and that it was untreatable. The infection had likely been caused by a small piece of food entering her lung because her MS no longer allowed her to have a cough reflex. The Doctors believed the infection had been brewing for some time. When she was told she was dying, she was also told she may have months or it may only be weeks. Nobody could say for sure.

Hanna had two things she wished for before she died. She said she wanted one last Christmas with her family and that she wanted to complete her book. Unfortunately, she didn't get either of these things in the literal sense but she did get a week at home surrounded by family and Christmas decorations, enjoying family dinners and traditional Christmas movies. It was family time that Christmas was really about for her so, in a sense, she had the Christmas she wished for. As far as finishing her book, we spent as much time as we could on it that last week but she was very weak and not able to speak for very long before becoming tired. I had talked to her about how she wanted the book to end and promised to finish it for her. A promise from a daughter to her dying Mom.

And so, a month after she passed peacefully out of this world, I now feel ready to keep this promise and continue the story for her. I know she wanted to end her family story with when she met and married my Dad. I think because her family dramatically changed with her moving out and getting married and so this story ended and a new one began.

I can tell you that things never improved with Edward. Hanna continued to have her alter egos deal with those traumatic occasions. So much so that, as an adult, Hanna didn't recall much of the abuse until she entered counselling and started having it all come out. At that point, she had a tough decision to make. She no longer wanted Edward in her life, as she now had children of her own to protect, but she still wanted to see her Mum who stood by Edward. Hanna chose to only see her Mum when Edward was not around. Unfortunately, this meant she saw much less of her Mum. To this day, nobody knows if Edward had a hand in any other suspicious activity that occurred in their neighborhood but his collection of newspaper clippings was definitely unusual.

Unfortunately, I can't fill in the gap between her Dad dying and her meeting my Dad. There weren't any stories/anecdotes during that time period that she shared with me.

I can however tell you how my parents great love story began.

. . . .

The earliest memory that Hanna had of Kyle was passing him in the hallways at their high school. Kyle was shy but would always say "Hi" to her in the halls as they passed. He was tall and blonde since he came from Scandinavian roots. Hanna was dating someone else during this time and so the conversation never went further than those hellos.

The next time their paths crossed was at a street dance in Victoria. It was set up on the road and lawns of the parliament buildings. Kyle spotted Hanna sitting on a curb with some of her girlfriends and couldn't help but notice how beautiful she was. Again, he walked over and said hello.

Then one day, Kyle was hanging out at a friend's place with a group of people and in came Hanna and her friend. They were there to hang out with the group as Hanna's boyfriend was busy doing something else. Some of the group started to play "Truth or Dare" and Kyle was asked, in front of a large group of curious teens, if he was a virgin. Kyle didn't even hesitate when he answered "Yes". This stuck with Hanna, as she was so impressed that he was comfortable enough with himself and honest enough to answer such a personal question at age 19.

It was shortly after this that Hanna and her boyfriend broke up. Apparently, the relationship had been barely hanging on for some time and they both realized it was time to end things. Hanna then began to think of Kyle and wonder what he might be up to. She started asking around and, eventually, it got back to Kyle that Hanna had been asking about him. He found out that Hanna was staying over at her friend's house, got the phone number and gave her a call there. Hanna agreed to go on a date with him, she would have been 16.

Many dates were to follow that first one. A couple that stand out in my Dad's mind (and mine from hearing the stories recounted over the years) were the dinner at the Bird House restaurant and a Horseback ride they took.

The night Kyle took Hanna to the Bird House was a challenging one for Hanna. You see, the Bird House was a nice restaurant at the very top of a downtown hotel. The views from the restaurant were spectacular as it overlooked downtown and the harbor. The trouble was the only way to get to it was by elevator. Hanna was very claustrophobic. So, as they arrived and she discovered they would have to take an elevator, she confided in Kyle that she didn't know if she could do it. He encouraged her and made her feel safe so she climbed in. When the doors closed, she buried her head in Kyle's shoulder and held her breath. Suddenly, the elevator stopped. Hanna panicked and started to scream as the doors opened. It had stopped on another floor to pick up more passengers. Needless to say, nobody entered and the doors closed. Kyle and Hanna continued to the top alone.

The day they went Horseback riding was the day Hanna decided that Kyle was "the one". While they were out riding, Kyle lost his wallet. It had wiggled its way out of his pocket with the motion of the horse but he wasn't sure where or when it had happened exactly. He had just been paid and his paycheck was in that wallet. They spent a bit of time looking for it and then Kyle said they should just forget about trying to find it and enjoy the rest of the day. The fact that Kyle could let this go so easily and not let it bring him down made Hanna sure she wanted to spend the rest of her life with him.

So, on a sunny summer day, when Kyle proposed to her on the lawns of the Parliament Buildings, Hanna said "YES!". It was a fitting place as he remembered seeing her there at the street dance and thinking how beautiful she was.

They were married when they were just 17 and 21. They went on to have 2 children and 3 grandchildren. Hanna was diagnosed with MS in her early 20s. She always said that she was taught not to stand up for herself as a child and just turn the other cheek to the hardships she faced. She felt the MS and ultimately being confined to the wheelchair was a metaphor for this "not being able to stand up for herself". She was forced to face the challenge of getting used to elevators and many other things along the way. Kyle and Hanna never gave up. They always found ways to make life go on happily. Their undying love for each other, optimistic attitudes and joy for life carried them through all challenges and they stayed happily married for 43 years until Hanna's passing.

Hanna inspired many people in her lifetime. Her courage, strength, determination and childlike spirit live on in her family and through her readers.

CPSIA information can be obtained
at www.ICGtesting.com
Printed in the USA
LVOW12s1523280717
542777LV00001B/23/P